277 Secrets
Your Snake ∧and Lizard
Wants You to Know

277 SECRETS
YOUR SNAKE and Lizard
WANTS YOU TO KNOW

Unusual and Useful
Information for Snake Owners
and Snake Lovers

PAULETTE COOPER

TEN SPEED PRESS
BERKELEY, CALIFORNIA

Ten Speed Press
P.O. Box 7123
Berkeley, California 94707
www.tenspeed.com

Distributed in Australia by Simon and Schuster Australia, in Canada by Ten Speed Press Canada, in New Zealand by Southern Publishing Group, in South Africa by Real Books, and in Southeast Asia by Berkeley Books.

Design by Lisa Patrizio

Library of Congress Cataloging-in-Publication Data
Cooper, Paulette.
277 secrets your snake and lizard wants you to know : unusual and useful information for snake owners and snake lovers / by Paulette Cooper.
     p. cm.
    ISBN 1-58008-035-9 (pbk.)
    1. Snakes as pets.   2. Lizards as pets.   I. Title.   II. Title: Two hundred seventy-seven secrets your snake and lizard wants you to know.
SF459.S5C66   1999
639.3'96—dc21   99-20517 CIP

First printing, 1999
Printed in Canada
1 2 3 4 5 6 7 8 9 10 – 02 01 00 99

Dedication

This book is dedicated to all the snake owners on the Internet Slither mailing list, with thanks for their secrets, suggestions, ideas, input, assistance, and contributions.

Contents

FOR LIZARD LOVERS
Be careful about letting your
lizard wander around on your rug.
Lizards can get rug fibers
wrapped around their toes, which
can cut off circulation, possibly
leading to the loss of a toe.

Acknowledgments

Helping me put all this together were: first, my talented writer friend, Sallie Batson, who assisted me with a few sections, and especially Peter Landau, a genius who has a way not only with words but with puns, and who helped with many chapters in the book.

I also want to thank my husband, Paul Noble, for his love and support throughout.

Mostly, I wish to thank (alphabetically) the snake (and lizard) owners who gave me so much help with this book, including checking many facts. Thanks especially to Lenny Flank, who answered so many questions cheerfully and quickly, and read this book prior to publication—twice. Also extremely helpful was Steve Grenard, as well as Charles Mosher, not to mention Sharon Bolton, Denise Loving, and Cynthia Merritt.

Also extremely helpful were those I interviewed besides the above. I wish to thank Zigi Blum, Dave Boeren, Christina Brewer, Leigh Carducci, Richard Cowan, Bill East, Dave Fulton, Bill Haast, John C. Haudensheild, Taryn L. Hook-Merdes, Esq., Valesa Linnean, Melissa Kaplan, Dave Karmann, Morgan Kennedy, Bill Love, Dr. Douglas Mader, Michele Mavity, Russ Megiveron, Ray Miller, Joe Norton, Jennifer Reynolds, Dan Sacco, Byron Sanford, Erik Stenstrom, Paul Weinberg, and John D. White.

And finally, on the editorial side, I wish to acknowledge Phil Wood, for whom I personally wrote this book; Jo Ann Deck, who makes writing all books for Ten Speed such a pleasure; and Aaron Wehner and Holly A. Taines, the super talented editors who were truly a pleasure to work with.

—Paulette Cooper

Introduction

What you are about to read is the most unusual and informative book ever written on the subject of snakes and lizards. It offers an enormous amount of material on a variety of unusual and useful topics, in the form of short zippy chapters that are easy and fun to read.

This book was written for those who own a snake or lizard and for those who do not. Of the hundreds of fascinating secrets, tips, findings, facts, and suggestions, many items are of general interest to anyone interested in snakes: for example, the chapters on dangerous snakes, snake sex, venom, crime, snake "speech," snake records, prejudices, etc.

But those who own snakes and lizards will find a lot of *practical* material for them as well—mostly in the second half of the book—on such subjects as ways to save money, ensure pet health, maintain vivariums, choose substrates, use food, eradicate parasites and diseases, and more.

Whichever group you're in, by the time you've finished, you'll have learned a lot about how snakes (and lizards) can live longer, healthier, and safer lives; how to understand what they're trying to tell you; and how you can be happier and safer with them—and vice versa—and much, much more.

These secrets and tips are based on the experience of dozens of snake (and lizard) owners, and knowledgeable experts, along with research material from books, newsletters, newspapers, journal articles, Internet newsgroups, and mailing list postings. In fact, this is the first snake book to disseminate the experience of snake and lizard owners on the Internet to other herpers.

Some of you have read my two earlier pet books: *277 Secrets Your Dog Wants You to Know* and *277 Secrets Your Cat Wants You to Know*, both written with my husband, Paul Noble. Paul and I constantly hear from readers who tell us that those books were the most interesting/informative/fun dog or cat books they ever read. I hope you will feel the same way about this one after you've finished.

Nobody Ever Tells You These Things, or the Lowdown on Snakes

How People are Tricked into Buying Nasty Snakes, and Other Dirty Tricks of Sellers

If you warm up to a cold snake, you might find yourself in hot water. Some breeders take what they call a "snake from hell," stop feeding it, and turn all the heating off until the snake is as listless as a piece of rope.

Then, when a likely looking customer (mark) comes around, the heartless seller tells him or her what a nice docile snake it is. The seller may even handle the snake to prove it, without handing it over to the potential buyer—who might become suspicious about handling a snake colder than a chilled cocktail.

The naive buyer takes the snake home, puts it in a tank at the proper temperature, and the snake soon returns to its old devilish ways—and is ravenous.

This trick was revealed by Ray Miller of Birmingham, who once bought what he thought was a docile corn snake. When he got it home and turned up the heat, he found that his snake had turned into a monster. Indeed, he called it "Carrie," after the Stephen King character—only no one would dare take this Carrie to the senior prom.

Even if a breeder means well, the temperature when you buy a snake can mask its true personality. Dave Fulton, who moderates the interesting Slither mailing list on the Internet, got a neonate Hogg Island boa at a herp show where the hall was warmish and the snakes on display had no heating.

When he got home, he "ended up having to pick up the snake with rawhide gloves," said Dave. "We called it 'Scargill,' after a militant British trade union leader, because like him, the snake would strike with the slightest provocation."

Two Other Dirty Tricks of Some Snake Sellers

Here are two other ways sellers con novice snake buyers. The first is based on the fact that captive-born snakes are usually more expensive and desirable than wild snakes, since the latter often have physical problems and make poorer pets. So, dishonest dealers say a snake is captive-born, when it was really captured in the wild.

How can you protect yourself from this scam? Look at the top of the snake's head. If the scales are discolored and dull, the snake may have suffered sun damage. Captive-bred snakes would probably not have been in the sun long enough to suffer any discernible effects from it.

Secondly, people have been defrauded in a more modern way. There's an expression that, on the Internet, no one knows if a person's a dog. Well, you also often don't know if someone's a "snake" either—or whether that's what the person is really selling.

Several people once purchased "animals" for sale cheaply on the Internet—only to receive rotting fruits and vegetables. The vendor was arrested, but these scammers have a habit of coming back, rather like the bad apples he was sending.

How can you protect yourself? Before buying a snake from a stranger, check out the Internet. Post questions about the seller on newsgroups or private mailing lists, like Slither, and find out what other people's experiences have been with that person. Chances are, if someone's been cheated by that seller, they aren't going to remain silent.

Do Snakes Like Music?

You've heard people sing "Snake your Booty"? No, wait, that's . . . Whatever. Snakes *do* seem to respond to musical vibrations, and some will actually come out to see what's happening when the music starts playing.

Especially if it's a band they like.

But just because they seem to be interested doesn't mean that they like what they "hear" (more likely feel). One rock group that was touring with some diamondbacks had to remove them because the loud sounds were causing them distress.

The fact that some snakes react badly to loud or bass music has been reported by many snake owners. One woman found that music from groups like Nine Inch Nails caused her snakes to slither around frantically and spiral into tight coils.

Sometimes, the response is even worse. One owner reported that once when he was jamming on his bass, his snake "came out of her hidey-hole" and defecated all over the front glass of her enclosure. "Everyone's a critic," he said philosophically.

SNAKE BITES
The most popular name for a pet python is "Monty."

If your snake seems to be bothered when you play music, you don't have to turn your CD, radio, TV, or whatever off, or even down. One herper—that is, someone who's interested in reptiles or amphibians—found it calmed her snakes when music was playing if she put her snakes' enclosures on computer mouse pads. These absorbed some of the offending vibrations. Or at least that's what she thinks, since her snakes stopped "complaining."

What's Wrong with the Movie Anaconda

Movies often make mistakes, but *Anaconda* started its long list of errors with something as basic as the patterns on the snake. What were they thinking? Here are a few more errors, caught by just one herper, David Boeren, a computer programmer in Atlanta who has been keeping snakes for six years.

- Follow the bouncing snake! The snake often looked like it was made of rubber.

- In one instance, the snake attacked someone tail first. (Snakes go after the heads of prey first.)

- The snake constantly disgorged its prey, so it could kill something else. (Snakes digest food slowly, sometimes taking weeks to finish off one meal.)

- At one point the bad guy was swallowed headfirst, and then disgorged headfirst. (Was the victim doing somersaults in the snake's guts?)

• In the shot of the anaconda swimming underwater, you can see the shape of the guide the snake just devoured in the snake's skin. (Doesn't the snake have bones? Did the man somehow slip out of the snake's rib cage?)

The mistakes were summarized by Byron Sanford from Germantown, Maryland, who owns a Burmese python: "It was a comedy."

Here She Comes: Miss Anaconda?

You think you've found a snake who's a real beauty? Does she look good in a bathing suit, play the piano, and recite a moving essay on the evils of pollution?

Even if the answer is no, if she can do her stuff in a skintight snakeskin suit like a pro, you could have entered her in the First North American Snake Beauty Pageant in 1997, run by the Georgia Herpetological Society.

There was no Miss Congeniality award, but several snakes were paraded across the runway by models, while an emcee described the species. Venomous snakes were kept in locked cages and voted on separately.

The judges' decision? The grayband won for the nonvenomous category, and the diamondback won for best-looking venomous snake. As herper Richard Cowan, who described this event, said: "I guess this shows that one of the 277 secrets a snake wants you to know is that snakes are beautiful creatures and are not slimy, unclean, or otherwise yucky."

Beau Ties, or How Snakes Make Love

You've heard the expression "I'm tied up with someone right now"? When snakes say that, they may really mean it. Snakes tie themselves into love knots, and these little tête-à-têtes—actually tail-à-tails—can last for hours, sometimes even more than a day. During this time, the romancing reptiles are actually having sexual intercourse, since the male's organ has protrusions or spines that fit into the female's cloaca, the reproductive and excretory orifice. But there's one other big difference between snake and human sex, mentioned in Klaus Griehl's book *Snakes: Giant Snakes and Non-Venomous Snakes in the Terrarium.* Unlike people, snakes don't move at all while they're mating. Well, unlike most people.

Here's where it gets really interesting. (You've been waiting, haven't you?) It was once believed that a snake had two half organs called hemipenis that together formed one, but it turns out that each "half" of the hemipenis is totally separate and can work independently. In other words, snakes have what's politely called "paired copulatory organs." Thus, the male snake has two penises—the dream of every man come true!

In some snakes, one of them just hangs around and doesn't do anything, but other snakes use both of them (not at the same time, of course). Some snakes are like right- and left-handed people, consistently using only one. Other snakes insert whichever organ is nearest the female. Some snakes alternate organs between successive matings with the same gal, and others alternate sex organs for each mating with different females.

Wow. However they do it, this is a really remarkable achievement, and it's amazing that snakes haven't become known for this, instead of some of their less exciting features, like forked tongues and fixed stares.

Now, if you're a guy, before you start thinking wistfully about these little creatures who make love all day and have two penises to use for their amorous escapades, here's a little fact that may make you less envious of them. In fact, it might make you cross your legs and think of Lorena Bobbitt.

FOR LIZARD LOVERS
Outdoor enclosures should not have glass or plastic walls, since sun traveling through the walls will increase their temperature.

In some species of snakes, if, say, the female decides to go left, and the male refuses to ask for directions and insists on turning right, according to a fun book called *Kinky Cats, Immoral Amoebas, and Nine-Armed Octopuses,* the male's hemipenis may break off. Ouch! ("Was it bad for you too?") But since the male has two of them, it isn't quite the total catastrophe it would be in some other species.

Why Snakes Have Two Sexual Organs

Is the purpose of their having two penises so that they can have twice the fun? Probably not. Two organs may be more effective than one for ensuring propagation of the species; in theory, doubling the odds.

One group of university scientists studied lizards, which are closely related and also blessed with two sexual organs. Their findings, reported in *New Scientist*, were that two sexual organs appeared to help the animal win out in sperm competition by keeping up a high level of production.

When alternating their penises in mating, the amount of ejaculate did not drop sharply, as would have happened if successive matings using the same organ took place.

Should You Get a Venomous Snake? or Some Like it Hot

You think you're tough. You want to impress your friends with your fearlessness. You think pit bulls are too passé or passive for you. You don't just keep *snakes*; you want venomous, or "hot" ones, as they're called. Keeping hot snakes is cool, you think. Think again.

Anyone who wants to get a venomous snake should listen to the advice of an expert in this area, like Erik Stenström of Sweden, who keeps and breeds cobras. If you're think of getting a venomous snake, he suggests, you should start off by acquiring a lot of experience with nonvenomous snakes first, because keeping hot snakes is not for beginners.

Also, get a mentor with years of experience to teach you, for example, how to handle certain tools—and yourself. If you're a bit off one day, it may not be a good time to handle your hot snake.

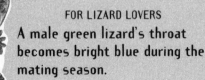

FOR LIZARD LOVERS
A male green lizard's throat becomes bright blue during the mating season.

What snakes are best to learn from? He suggests you choose problem ones: bad snakes; antisocial miscreants; snakes that refuse to eat; that shed poorly; or have mites or throat rot. Why? Because it's best to make a mistake with a snake that can only give you a bad bite, instead of a rush to the emergency room, possibly followed by the morgue.

If you're so inclined (as to not decline possibly being reclined), you should also start your hot snake experience with a snake that is only mildly venomous. Then, if you're bitten, you'll have a "learning" experience rather than an out-of-the-body experience.

If you're still truly committed to owning a hot variety of snake (remembering that they are not pets and should be treated as such), do your homework and get a snake you're capable of taking care of—or it'll take care of you. "You can never be prepared enough," Erik said, "A bite is going to happen. The odds are all in the snake's favor."

Is This Snake Hot Enough for You?

Lenny Flank, who has been keeping reptiles for over twenty years, says in *Snakes: Their Care and Keeping* that, if you want a venomous snake, you should pick up a "really really nasty [nonvenomous] critter and keep it for about a year. Every time the little sucker gets a tooth in you, write yourself a note saying: 'I could be dead right now, and if I survive, I'll owe the hospital around $35,000 or so.' Tape it to your snake cage. After a year, decide if you really want to keep a dangerously venomous snake."

Steve Grenard, an author and expert in venom and snakebites, reminds people that, "Venomous snakes are *not* guns. But they're like playing Russian roulette with five bullets in the chamber and just one empty, as opposed to the other way around. I am sure no competent gun person would ever play Russian roulette in either configuration."

Can a Snake Watch TV?

Even if snakes could watch TV, would they, with all the crummy shows that are on? Apparently some would, like the snake who disappeared in Arizona and was later found curled up in front of his owner's TV, calmly watching *America's Most Wanted*. (He was probably checking to see if there was a segment on about his disappearance.)

Did the snake enjoy the show? Since snakes can't separate stationary objects from their background and can't really perceive shapes—images are not sharply defined for them—they probably can't see much.

Let's say one was watching NBC and the peacock was frequently featured. A snake might have been able to see the bright colors of the peacock's plume, since snakes have both rods and cones in their retinas and can therefore probably see colors. But they would not be able to see the peacock itself unless it moved.

FOR LIZARD LOVERS
There's a photo on the Internet of a python, with a swollen belly, that has supposedly just eaten a man.

If they were watching *Seinfeld*, though, since snakes are sensitive to movement, they would have been able to see Kramer when he stumbled into Seinfeld's apartment. But since snakes' eyesight isn't so great, they probably wouldn't have seen Maris in *Frasier*. Then, too, neither could the audience. Furthermore, snakes can't hear much of anything, so they wouldn't have heard any of the jokes on TV—such as they are—or the sound track. Which could have been a blessing.

So all in all, unless one of their relatives is on the Discovery Channel, snakes are probably better off staying home and playing with the mice, or reading a good book—like this one.

Snake Eyes, or Do Snakes Ever Sleep?

Even though snakes don't have eyelids and can't close their eyes, they *do* sleep, although it may be hard to tell exactly when it's happening. Sometimes it's easier to tell that they *have* been sleeping, as they may startle or jerk after a period of extreme immobility.

Signs that a snake is actually in the process of sleeping include constriction of its pupils, tucking of its head into its coils, or burrowing in its substrate. (Not to mention getting into bed, sinking its head into the pillow, and pulling up the covers.)

One final method of determining somnolence: Wave your hand around within the snake's field of vision. If there's no eye movement, and no tongue flicks, it's sleeping—or just totally bored by your ridiculous behavior.

Tricks for Opening Your Snake's Mouth

Need to open a snake's mouth to give it some medicine—or maybe just to see it open its mouth and go "aaahhh"? Here are a few ways:

- If you've got a small snake, take a folded business card, or if it's a large snake, a folded paper plate, and put it in the snake's mouth. Paper products are good because they're soft, can be easily disposed of afterward so they don't need to be disinfected, and the fold keeps the snake from getting paper cuts.

- A ballpoint pen can be used to poke open the front of a snake's mouth. Once the snake opens wide, put the pen in its mouth crosswise to hold it open.

- A rubber spatula works. If you need to give your snake medication, you can pop it right behind the spatula.

Finally, on the Slither Internet mailing list, someone jokingly suggested that the best way to get a snake to open its mouth may be to sit with it in front of your computer and enter a chat room. Then, take advantage of the snake's open mouth as it begins to yawn from the not-so-scintillating conversation.

Chew on This for a While

Here are three interesting facts about snake's teeth.

- Snakes have recurved teeth, facing backward. Trying to wedge your fingers into the corners of their mouths if they bite you can result in your getting pricked with the rearmost teeth—and the snake possibly clenching its jaws more tightly.

- Snakes cannot use their teeth to chew or break up prey. The teeth help hold prey and push it into the throat. The teeth have been described as being like grappling hooks; while their stomach juices aid them with digestion.

- Some snakes have as many as 200 teeth, a lot more than people.

Snakes Get in Your Hair (and on Your Glasses)

Snake owners who wear glasses or have long hair sometimes sadly discover that their small snakes confuse their glasses for a ladder to reach their hair; or their snakes think glasses are a toy to knock off, or a nice place to sit on, peer down from, hang from, or hang out in.

Generally, such serpentine games are harmless to owner and snake, although one snake who slipped through someone's hair right after it was freshly dyed came out covered in green streaks.

Color aside, though, a snake on one's head can be uncomfortable, especially when the snake is large—like over five feet—and heavy, and fancies spending hours curled up on top of its owner's head, as if it were an Indian turban. Besides, who wants to look like Medusa?

> **FOR LIZARD LOVERS**
> Don't use fine sand in a desert terrarium, since the grains can cake between the lizard's scales, cling to food, and clog up their intestines.

Some owners have found that braiding their hair helps keep their snakes away, although some small snakes still like to slip into that tiny area at the very top of the braid. One woman who put her hair into dreadlocks reported no better success; her "do" didn't mean "don't" for her snake.

Another woman who washed her hair in vinegar found her snake did indeed hate it, but so did everyone else who went near her. Her friends preferred to be with someone who had a snake on her head than someone who smelled like a salad.

So far, the one thing that has been reported to work: One woman brushes her hair right before she takes her snakes out, and her snakes don't seem to like her hair as much then.

> **SNAKE BITES**
> There's a cartoon character named "Julius Squeezer."[®]

Now, if she could just figure out what to do with her glasses.

Can You Catch Mites from Your Snakes?

Yes. In a paper presented more than twenty years ago, and reported in *Medical Herpetology*, Dr. H. Bernard Bechtel related the case of a mother and three children who were all itchy and infested with some type of snake mite.

It turned out they owned a python, who liked to sit on their upholstered chair—which was found to be infested with this mite.

Treating the chair solved the problem.

FOR LIZARD LOVERS

The most popular lizard in America and Canada is the green iguana lizard—more than one million of them were imported last year. But they're also the most frequently thrown away pet of the nineties, for during their twenty-year life span, iguanas never stop growing. An adorable six-inch baby can become a nasty three-foot adult in two years. Furthermore, an adult iguana can move faster than most people.

Single Snakes and the Differences between Boas and Girls

Macho Macho Snake

Forget any notion about tender, loving snakes, especially in the males. Before and during mating, the male may bite the female's neck, or butt his hopeful partner-to-be if she's reluctant to join him. Afterward, although some snakes, such as the male diamond python, may stay with one female for a month or more during the breeding season, most snakes do not hang around after mating (like some male human "snakes").

Occasionally, however, a male snake may stay with the same female for a short while before the mating, but he generally does so with ulterior motives. Most likely, he just wants to be ready the instant she is. Afterward, when the breeding female is no longer receptive, the male snake, having loved 'em, leaves 'em, and slithers off into the night, or day, never to see his one-night stand again.

If a little baby snake (or dozens) comes along, the female can't count on the responsible male to be a good "father" either. But she's unlikely to throw a hissy fit over her deadbeat dad leaving her with the diapers and a needy snakelet, since she's not such a hot mother either, often not hanging around for long after she gives birth.

In fact, it isn't known, whether either the mother or father even recognizes his or her own "kids" later. This gives them a perfectly legitimate excuse to ignore them if junior comes to them later for college money. ("I'm your *what?*")

FOR LIZARD LOVERS
According to Herp Help by Lenny Flank Jr., male lizards have large pores on the inside of their thighs, which secrete a waxy substance that helps the male grip the female during mating.

Are Some Male Snakes Stalkers and Stealers and Poseurs?

It was reported by Chris Mattison, author of several great books on snakes, including the comprehensive *Encyclopedia of Snakes*, that some male snakes will track down and follow a "ripe" female for several days, even weeks. That kind of stalking behavior in people could get them put away!

Even odder animal behavior (also encountered in the human species) is for a male snake to act like a female one. The common garter snake, for example, sometimes causes a competitive male to come on to him. Then, whoops, he slips in and steals the lady. (Now this guy's a real snake.)

Some males will also steal already-paired females from their partners. Even though he isn't part of a couple, a lonely male with no date on Saturday night will sometimes hang around a group of snakes, and then bam—the lonely loser sneaks in and steals a little love from the lady while her chosen partner is busy with various precoital preparations, like "strangling" the competition.

Snake Courtship, or a Hiss Is Just a Hiss

Since a male snake can't tell a female snake what's on his mind, he has to let her know in other ways when he's in the mood for love. He may rub his chin or head over the lower part of her back, flick his tongue over her skin, or even tap on her back. (*"Excuse me, miss, but are you busy right now?"*)

If he has vestigial limbs, he may use them to tickle her, or ride on her back, making jerking movements as she crawls along. (When she screams, "Get off my back," she may mean it literally.)

Although males are sometimes pretty obvious in their desires, females are more subtle in letting males know when they're receptive to the male's crude and lewd advances. Female snakes have scent trails, emanating not only from their anal glands, but also from their skin. "New" skin seems to attract males, so it isn't only humans who do better with the opposite sex after they've put on some fresh, clean clothes.

How to Get Snakes in the Mood for Love

If you decide that you want to breed two snakes, you may have to get them to agree with you. Here are some tips on how to do that (without dimming the lights and putting on Frank Sinatra records), offered by author Klaus Griehl:

- Keep them thin. Fat, overfed snakes often aren't interested in sex. Does this remind you of anything?

- Separate the snakes and then reunite them at mating season.

- Two snakes who live together in a terrarium often aren't interested in breeding with each other. Join or form a club with other herpetologists, so you can borrow another sexually mature snake.

- Keep snakes at the right temperature and humidity (varies from species to species).

How to Tell the Difference between the Boas and the Girls

Since female snakes can't put on lipstick or high heels, males must rely on other cues to determine who is worth crawling after. For snakes, it's not that difficult to determine who is the fairer sex, for at the base of the snakes' tails are musk glands, with distinctive scents emanating from the females.

While it's easy for snakes to tell the difference, how do snake owners know which is the boy and which is the girl, without going around sniffing

FOR LIZARD LOVERS

If your lizard is separating out the food it prefers with its snout, finely chop its favorite food before mixing it in with the other food to get your lizard to eat everything. Another trick: Make it a "burrito" with the greens your lizard likes as the shell, and the blended vegetables it doesn't like as the inside.

their pets? Fortunately, there are visual and clinical ways to tell the difference, although unfortunately, they're not always that accurate or clear-cut.

For example, while occasionally the male snake's head is bigger, the bodies of male snakes are often (but not always) smaller than those of females of the same species—sometimes by several feet—since females need more room in their lower bodies to hold eggs or live young.

There are also usually differences in the size of the tails and spurs. Male snakes tend to have longer thicker tails to house the hemipenis. And, if the snakes have spurs (small claws) on the side, as do boas, the spurs are smaller in females.

SNAKE BITES
The American Revolution flag with the motto "Don't Tread on Me," was a reference to rattlesnakes.

In addition to sexual organs and appendages, there may also be differences in the number of scales on the snakes, although it may be hard to examine these on wiggling animals. Some snake owners wait for a snake to shed and then count and compare the scales to those of other snakes whose sex is known.

Other than looking, the standard clinical way to tell sexual difference in snakes is by "probing," or inserting a thin shaft into the tail, by way of the cloaca. This has to be done very carefully or a snake can be damaged. Furthermore, the results are not always conclusive. But if the snake is a male, the probe generally goes in deeper than it would inside a female of the same size and species.

Some people also try to determine sex manually, by "popping" the male snake, also called "tail-kinking," which sounds dirtier than it is. To pop a snake, you turn it upside down and gently roll your thumbs where the snake's organ should be. The pressure on the tail causes the hemipenis—which is kept inverted until needed—to be turned inside out. If it pops out, the snake's a boy. If it doesn't, the snake's a girl—or maybe it was done wrong. Popping should be done cautiously, so as not to hurt the snake—or come up with the wrong answer.

Finally, you can ask your veterinarian to give your snake a blood test to determine the presence of hormones. But that's not nearly as interesting as the other methods.

Go Climb a Tree

What happens if two snakes are at it, and one gets tired and wants to call it quits? If there's some disagreement over the direction in which the romance is going while the snakes are literally locked together, since snakes don't have arms and hands with which to pull the other, the male may simply drag the female along with his organ.

Snakes have been spotted in *flagrante delicto,* dragging an unenthusiastic partner around. In one case, reported in *Journal of Herpetology*, a male racer pulled some poor female snake sixteen feet up a tree with him. What a drag!

You've Got Male!

Talk about girl power! Some snakes have shown the ability to reproduce without males! While this situation has been reported in only a smattering of snakes, such as the Brahminy blind snakes and, more rarely, the timber rattlesnake and wandering garter snake, it may happen among other snakes as well.

Zoos generally keep snakes and other animals in pairs; thus, whenever a little one comes along, people assume it happened because the couple was doing what comes naturally. In fact, though, what happened could occasionally be a very unnatural parthenogenic birth. Of course, some cases of what was thought to be parthenogenesis in the past could have been sperm retention.

The *Rocky Mountain News* told the story of a Colorado man who discovered a couple of years ago that his fourteen-year-old timber rattlesnake had given birth to a son—in most animals parthenogenic births can only produce females—which he called Napoleon.

The man had raised the mother snake—whom he named Marsha Joan—since she was two days old, and he knew she had never been with a male. The owner is still trying to figure this one out, which appears to be a rare instance of spontaneous mutation. (Or at least that's what Marsha Joan is trying to convince him is what happened.)

Snake "Chastity Belts"

Many species have ways of preventing more than one male from fertilizing an egg. For example, the human egg becomes almost entirely impermeable to another sperm once impregnation has occurred.

Some snakes have their own little trick for this as well. In some species, if the female mates with more than one male, the baby snakes will have more than one father. This is called superfecundation, and is common in many animal species.

A few snakes that prefer a more traditional arrangement have come up with their own way of ensuring that, after they impregnate a female snake, another snake doesn't come along and get the credit—or the baby. Once again, Chris Mattison is the one who revealed this interesting information in his book: *The Encyclopedia of Snakes*. It seems that some possessive male snakes actually plug up the female after mating, producing what are sort of snake-style "chastity belts." To make these, the male secretes a fluid that he deposits into the female immediately after he has placed his sperm in her. After a few minutes, the fluid hardens, forming a barrier to further impregnation by other males. "That way, no other male can replace, commingle, or dilute his sperm."

FOR LIZARD LOVERS
If you freeze your lizard's food, add brewer's yeast to it before feeding your lizard, since freezing may make the food lose some of its vitamins.

Storing It Up, or the Seven Year Itch

Some female snakes don't have to copulate each time they have a clutch; they can store the sperm in them from previous matings for as long as seven years. Then, because of sperm retention, they can refertilize themselves each year with the original sperm, without breeding again.

Can you image what these gals say to a male if they're not in the mood to mate? "Not this year, darling, I have a headache."

Snake Pen Pals, or Does Your Snake Have the Write Stuff?

Did anyone send your snake a birthday card this year? Is something missing from its life? Sure, you love your snake, but that's not the kind of love it's missing. It needs companionship of its own kind, a relationship more intimate than you can offer.

Perhaps you didn't realize this problem existed for your snake, but an agency in Spain, on the romantic Mediterranean coast, thinks that deep down, though, snakes want to bond with other slithery soul mates, and that your troubled, lovelorn snake can easily be made happy with their help.

This agency, appropriately called Happy Animals, has formed the world's first animal matchmaking service, and claims to be able to find the perfect mate for your friend.

At the moment, they're only talking about four-legged pets, but they have plans to branch out soon into the no-legged ones, bringing romance to reptiles seeking reproduction, or at least companionship for those cold lonely nights in their vivarium.

FOR LIZARD LOVERS
Never pick up a lizard by the tail, since many species shed their tails.

Once you sign up, your snake will be added to a database that includes the snake's best features, a photograph, and a short description of the qualities it (or you) is looking for in a life partner.

Who knows? They say there's a mate for everyone who walks the earth; maybe there's one for those who glide too.

Dancing in the Dark

Some snakes seem to do a sort of dance, and no one's quite sure exactly why they do it or even *what* they're doing, and what role it plays in the mating. But the male serpentine dance, more snaking a leg than shaking a leg, is probably done to impress the female, or fight for her, or drive other males away, or assert the male's dominance, or all of the above.

For example, the *Beastly Book* describes how a male diamondback will climb up on a female and then collapse gradually and wrestle, repeating this ritual many times. Or two water moccasins will glide along, twisted together, and cross and recross their necks. During this "dance," the smaller snake circles the larger one, touches it with his tongue and snout, and together they rise higher out of the water, sometimes continuing this for an hour. It sounds like more fun than the Macarena!

What to Expect When Your Snake Is Expecting

Here are a few things to expect if your snake is about to give birth, or already has. Most of them are not true all of the time for all snakes, but it's better to have a general idea of what might happen, than to be unhappily surprised or confused when it is too late.

- Expect some snakes to give birth to a full-formed snake, and others to hatch eggs.

- Expect small snakes to have small clutches.

- Expect the egg to become a little smaller right before it hatches. Shells often shrivel slightly as the hatchling snarfs up the yolk.

- Expect hatchlings to take several days to slice through (pip) the egg. Some snakes like to stay inside the egg for awhile, absorbing the yolk. Aren't there days when you don't want to get out of bed right away either?

- Expect that you may have to help open some of the eggs, if the babies haven't poked their heads out to breathe.

• Expect that some eggs will stick together. They're supposed to in some species.

• Expect pythons to incubate their eggs by wrapping themselves around the freshly laid eggs and "shivering," which warms the eggs. She's not cold; she's a mommy.

• Don't expect the eggs to be brittle. They're leathery.

• Expect some snakes to occasionally eat their young. It's the exception for most, but it's still one reason why you should generally remove the eggs after the mother has hatched them.

• Expect the little tyke to be aggressive if the parent is. Since they get no postnatal support from their parents, they must be able to hunt immediately in the wild.

• Expect the babies to have their first shed within a few days after birth.

A Rolling Stone Gathers No (Sphagnum) Moss, and Should You Use It Too?

Sphagnum moss was used as a sterile dressing for wounds during the Civil War, but now, many herpeticulturists use it as an incubation medium or nesting site on which snakes can lay their eggs.

According to *Carnivorous Plant Newsletter*, however, long-fiber dried sphagnum moss has recently been implicated in causing a fungal disease called *sporotrichosis*. Since treatment for this disease is extended and unpleasant, be careful, and stay tuned for any other current findings in this area. (And just to be on the safe side, you might want to avoid all Civil War reenactments. You can never be too cautious.)

Bingo! Snake Eggs, or the Yolk's on You

Someone stealing snake eggs is already a bizarre story, but add to this the fact that the person who did it was trying to divine winning lottery numbers from them—and that it was a monk!—and you've got a real doozy.

Reuters reported that a Buddhist monk in eastern Thailand stole the unhatched eggs of two rare snakes, believing they would enable him to guess the last three digits of a government lottery. (Why he believed this about the eggs was a bit scrambled at press time.)

Apparently he wasn't the only one who gave credence to this weird notion. So many tourists came to see the eggs in their original exhibit, also thinking they could divide the winning numbers, that the police had to put up a barbed-wire fence around the exhibit to safeguard it. The monk, incidentally, returned the eggs after being threatened with legal action. Perhaps he thought he didn't have an egg to stand on.

FOR LIZARD LOVERS

Although some lizards like dog food, it's not good for them (although it may be good for crickets, which are fed to some lizards). And don't feed cat food to a lizard, since cat food is high in fat and reptiles don't digest fat well.

Gotcha! Dangerous Snakes, or Read This Before It's Too Late*

*If you are bitten by a venomous snake, stop reading and go to a doctor immediately. This is the only excuse you have for putting down this book.

Nine Fascinating Facts about Venomous Snakes You Don't Want to Learn Firsthand

- *Using their heads.* Some snake venom can continue to flow even after the snake's head has been chopped off. Such "spasms" can deliver a full amount of venom and be as bad as a bite from a live snake.

- *"Hot" but not bothered.* Many people never feel a venomous snake biting them.

- *Just a bit off the old block.* Baby snakes are usually as venomous as their parents, even if the baby has just been born. For example, when a baby cobra is less than an inch thick and a foot long, its venom is as potent as its parents'.

- A person may suffer more seriously from the venom if the snake bites them to attack them than if the snake bite is a defensive reaction to, say, a person mistakenly stepping on the snake.

- Many people bitten by strongly venomous snakes are not that badly injured, since the snake may not get much skin in its mouth. Also, the snake may not be able to chew for long, which would give it more time to empty itself of its venom.

- Even venomous snakes don't always inject venom in their bites.

- Some venom is species specific and only acts on certain prey.

- Most snakes inject a lot more venom than they need to kill their prey.

- Technically, snake venom doesn't come from their mouths. It's produced in glands located in back of the snake's eyes.

Fangs for Nothing

- *Spring forward; you fall back.* The fangs of most vipers are retractable and spring forward when they attack, so the prey is almost injected.

- *Dig this!* Most fangs are set back a bit in the mouth and there is an empty space in front of them so the snake can drive its fangs into its prey deeper.

- *Back up!* It takes longer for the venom to take effect on its victim if it comes from snakes with back fangs than front-fanged snakes.

- Fangs in vipers and pit vipers are so long they have to be folded against the roof of the mouth or the snake wouldn't be able to close its jaws.

- Fangs have holes in them, for injecting the venom.

- Front-fanged snakes use their fangs like hypodermic needles and inject their venom. Most rear-fanged snakes use their venom after they have already seized their victim. The venom drips down into the wound, numbing their prey so that it stops struggling as it is being swallowed.

What's the Most Dangerous Snake in the World?

A snake expert was once asked what he thought was the most dangerous snake in the world. His reply: "Are you asking for the snake that bites the most people, kills the most people, or the one I would least want to be locked in a phone booth with?"

Part of the problem in choosing which is the most dangerous snake is that everyone has varying criteria, and different definitions of "dangerous." Some experts consider only the power of the venom, although not all bites are equal, and the amount of venom may differ slightly from day to day in the same snake for the same type of prey.

> **FOR LIZARD LOVERS**
> If you have a tree-dwelling or climbing lizard, you should have very tall plants.

In fact, even the method of testing the strength of the venom may be invalid, because the standard way, milking a snake, doesn't equal the amount of venom injected by a snake in a normal bite.

Some base a snake's dangerousness on its size (sometimes in conjunction with the potency of the venom); the fang's size; the likelihood that you

> **FOR LIZARD LOVERS**
> Don't feed lizards alfalfa sprouts; the sprouts may contain salmonella.

will encounter the snake; the likelihood of recovering from a bite; or the "venom yield" or fatalities per bite, in other words, the chances that if you are bitten that you will die, etc.

Not surprisingly, considering the different criteria, several snakes are often cited as the most dangerous. Two that crop up on most lists are the saw-scaled viper and the inland taipan. The former kills more people because of complicated and difficult to control hemorrhage problems, and the latter has the deadliest venom of any known land snake on a drop-for-drop basis. Although, if you're including sea snakes, the *Guinness Book of Records* says, "Hydrophis belcheri [which] has a myotoxic venom a hundred times as toxic as that of the Australian Taipan . . . whose bite can kill a man in minutes."

Other snakes chosen as the most dangerous generally include the eastern (Australian) brown snake, the puff adder, the Gaboon viper, yellow-bellied sea snake, beaked sea snake, Russell's viper, hook-nosed snake, Malayan pit viper, fer-de-lance, Dubois's reef sea snake, Malayan or common krait, tiger snake, coral snake, boomslang, Cape cobra, king cobra, bushmaster, death adder, and the green or black mamba.

The Fierce Snake and Saw-Scaled Viper, or Tough Snakes Don't Dance

The inland taipan, in Australia called the "fierce snake," earns its moniker, for its venom is said to be able to kill 250,000 white mice—and perhaps 100 people—with just one bite. Fortunately, most people don't have to go out of their way to avoid the taipans, since they are found only in a remote section of Australia.

Steve Irwin, known as the "Crocodile Hunter" in his native Australia, not only found one, but for a Discovery special on dangerous snakes of Australia, he lay down on the ground while one swished up and tasted his cheek! Luckily for him, the snake apparently didn't like what it tasted and left.

The saw-scaled viper is found throughout the Middle East, and Steve Grenard says that during the Gulf War, allied troops were rightly more afraid of encountering a saw-scaled viper than the enemy. He says that this snake is the most dangerous snake, if you consider the percentage of people who die from its bite.

"Two Steps" to Death, or Come Let us Prey

Most snakebites are not going to kill you almost instantaneously, but certain snakes are occasionally referred to as "two-step," "three-step," or "five-step" snakes.

What this means is that, after someone has been bitten, they can supposedly only walk two or three or five steps before they're a dead man walking or, by that point, a dead man falling.

These phrases became popular in Vietnam, where the troops were generally referring to the yellow-headed kraits, common kraits, banded kraits, and the Asian cobra.

Just one more reason why the Vietnam War sucked.

How Snakes Eat Prey—Including People

Do snakes make pigs of themselves? Sometimes, since they may eat more than 1½ times their own weight, which is rather like a 150-pound person gulping down a 225-pound meal. (Some women would gladly do that if they were eating chocolate.) The rule of thumb is that snakes can swallow anything up to three times the diameter of the thickest part of their body, which is akin to a person swallowing a beach ball. (Don't try to prove this.)

How can snakes gorge like this? A king snake, for example, will carefully fold the meal inside its stomach as it swallows. But how do snakes get the food in their mouths in the first place?

For most snakes, opening their mouths wide to take a gargantuan bite isn't a problem. While humans can only open their mouths to a 30-degree angle, some snakes can go as far as 130 degrees.

Now, you're going to need a strong stomach to read the following—just as a snake needs a strong stomach to do it.

Swallowing is made easier for snakes because they eat their prey head-first, folding the prey's limbs to the sides. The snakes can also cover their meal with saliva, making the food go down easier. Snakes swallow their prey whole, and they ultimately digest everything, including the bones. Are you OK so far? To continue. . . .

FOR LIZARD LOVERS
Clip your lizard's nails under very bright light to avoid cutting the vein, which is usually a dark line running through the nails.

Pulitzer Prize-winning author Jared Diamond wrote in *Discovery* magazine about a fourteen-year-old Indonesian boy who was swallowed by a reticulated python. The boy was still recognizable in the snake's stomach when the snake was killed and cut open two days later. Indeed, he was found with his legs crossed, his left hand wedged between his legs, and his right arm bent behind his head.

"Picture how it might feel to be slowly forced headfirst down a python's throat, drowning in its saliva, with your arms pinioned at your sides by the grip of its cheek muscles," he wrote.

Indeed.

Here's Spit in Your Eye

Watch out for some snakes—like certain species of cobras—who, when threatened, if they can't get their fangs into you, will spit venom at you just as soon as look at you. In fact, they'll spit venom *while* they're looking at you, from as far as seven feet away, with incredible accuracy.

A spit in the eye can be more than embarrassing: It can lead to painful burning, conjunctivitis, and possibly even blindness. Still, before you cry over spilled venom, there is a remedy. If it happens to you (God forbid), splash the infected eye liberally with water, saline solution, milk, or any other bland solution. (One or two adrenaline drops are also supposedly effective.)

Whatever you do, don't do what you will most want to do. Don't rub your eyes. This may enable the venom to enter your bloodstream through the mucous membranes, and the blindness may then be permanent.

And, oh yes, don't forget: Slowly move away from a spitting snake, so it can't add injury to the spit by biting you too.

Do Snakes Ever Attack—or Kill—Themselves?

Yes, both can happen. For example, one man gave his pet snake, Wheezer, a live rat to eat. The snake accidentally broke the rat's nose, causing the rat to bleed profusely. When some of the blood dripped on the snake, Wheezer clamped down on his own body three times before he finally seemed to realize he was chomping on himself.

The most famous case of a snake accidentally biting and killing itself occurred in 1963. A Gaboon viper bit its own back at the Philadelphia Zoo, and died, supposedly from "traumatic injury to a vital organ"—not from its own venom.

Does Red Touch Yellow Really Kill a Fellow?

If you're interested in snakes (and if you're not, why are you reading this book?), you've probably heard the jingle: "Red touch yellow kills a fellow." Created by early colonists, this jingle was used by people in the southeastern United States to spot the venomous coral snake. But just because it rhymes, does it mean it's right?

According to *Reptiles* magazine, yes, in some places. West of the Mississippi, the red-touch-yellow mnemonic device doesn't always differentiate the venomous snake from the harmless variety. Then, you'll have to look at the head to tell if you should stay or go. The coral snake has a black snout, while non-venomous snakes' are brightly ringed in reds, yellows, or whites.

But rules were made to be broken, and this one can be trashed if you venture south of the border. For instance, in Mexico, tropical American coral snakes don't all have black noses.

No one has yet been able to come up with a rhyme for that.

How to Keep Young Children and Dangerous Snakes Apart

Many people are concerned about having snakes around their children, despite the fact that, if a snake owner is careful, his or her children are far more likely to undergo a cat- or dog-related injury, if they are also in the house.

Still, certain precautions should be taken where snakes are concerned, so unnecessary accidents can be avoided. Christina Brewer, owner of eleven boids (boas and pythons)—some as long as eighteen feet and as heavy as 200 pounds—reveals how she keeps her four-year-old son and his friends from the snakes, and vice versa:

- She keeps the big snakes in a locked basement room.
- The small snakes are in latched cages.
- The snakes are too high for little ones to reach without assistance.
- When the toddlers handle any of the snakes, someone controls the head.
- The children must wash their hands and arms when they are done.

Do Snakes Really Go for Babies?

Many of the victims of snakebites have been infants and young children, which might not be an accident. Snakes may specifically target the younger set.

For example, in one publicized instance, a snake went straight for a baby who was asleep between his mother and father, skipping the parents sleeping on both sides of the child.

Dr. David Chizar, an expert on how snakes go after their prey, established that snakes are drawn to blood and amniotic fluid from pregnant mice, suggesting that they might be more interested in pregnant women, and babies who have just been born, than in older prey.

Babies do have a unique smell, and there is evidence that all animals, not just snakes, are attracted to blood. So, ironically, those old wives' tales about snakes and babies may have a grain of truth in them.

Everything Interesting You Want to Know about (Ouch) Snakebites and (Gasp) Constriction

The Worst Place to Get Bitten by a Snake

All right, the worst place to get bitten (or squeezed) by a snake is *any* place, especially if it's your place. But seriously, where on your body do you not want to be bitten? Yes, of course there. But also . . . if you're squeamish, stop now. OK, you have been warned.

Dr. Charles Mosher, a snake educator and retired electrical engineer in Menlo Park, California, says the worst place to get bitten is on the eyeball. If this scares you—and hopefully you thought about the possibility before reading this because otherwise this is just going to give you one more thing to worry about—get yourself some plastic OSHA safety goggles, if you don't ordinarily wear glasses. (If safety glasses seem too flimsy, perhaps a welder's helmet.)

What about constriction? Experts say the worst place for that to happen is around your diaphragm. Most constricting snakes in the wild won't wrap themselves around your arm, because they're not really interested in doing a blood pressure reading. No, it's your chest that's in danger, especially since a snake's technique is to tighten each time the victim exhales. And if the victim struggles, well, the snake just wraps harder. Cute, eh?

> **SNAKE BITES**
> It was probably a Russell's viper that Arthur Conan Doyle was referring to in his story "The Speckled Band."

Where does this end? Once the snake senses no heartbeat, it begins to swallow its prey—whole. Incredibly, the snake rarely breaks any bones, and the person pretty much retains their original shape afterwards. Not that it'll do them much good.

Five Tricks to Avoid Being Bitten and the Most Common Causes of Snakebites

Sharon Bolton is always filled with good ideas, based on her experience with eighteen snakes (not to mention five cats, three dogs, a canary, and other assorted animals). She suggests the first three ways below that you can avoid being bitten by a snake that you're handling.

Getting the hook: "Handle the snake with a hook, especially with all venomous snakes, for all activities, when removing it from the cage."

An apple a day keeps the snake away: "Spray bitter apple on your hands and arms before handling a snake. The taste will discourage the snake from repeating its biting. (Although apples might not help you the first time.)"

Pillow talk: "Put your hand in a pillowcase and handle the snake through that."

Dress for success: "Get a pair of very thin cotton or gardening gloves— maybe even a long-sleeved shirt—and wear them when you're handling a snake," she says.

And speaking of gloves, Dave Fulton says that rubber gloves work well with a smallish snake that is "a bit nippy. These give a good 'feel' and grip well, but their major benefit is that the rubber tastes absolutely foul to the snake, and I'm assured they rarely bite more than twice."

Here's more on the bill of bites. These precautions may help prevent the type of bite called an "illegitimate bite," one received when handling (or approaching) a snake for work, or play, while attempting to catch it, etc.

The other type of bite is called, not surprisingly, a "legitimate bite," which is accidentally received by people who just happen to be unlucky enough to be in the area of the snake. The end result is the same: It sucks to get bitten by a snake. If you make the following mistakes, it may very well happen:

- If you've just handled food and then touch a snake, when the snake smells the food on your warm hand, it may confuse your hand with prey and strike it. This is especially likely to occur among those who feed their snakes live rodents.

- If you wake snakes up when they're still sleeping, they might strike. Shh, let them sleep.

- Showing nervousness or fear may cause a snake to strike. A snake senses both and doesn't like it one bit. (Or could that be one bite?)

Watch Out for Perfume!

Some snakes despise perfume—especially perfumes containing the musk of the civet cat—so much that they may even strike at the glass when a person wearing the foul odor comes nearby. Talk about everybody being a critic.

"My boas will go into a rage when they smell any of those musky heavy perfumes of the sort that drive people off elevators," says one snake owner.

Which perfumes are these? Some snakes are reported to hate JOOP. The other? One snake owner posted that her daughter once worked at Victoria's Secret, and when she wore their perfume and came near her snake afterward, "It immediately tried to bite her in the face."

Maybe that's Victoria's secret.

How to Avoid Snakes in the Wild, or None Like It Hot

People reading this book are likely to be *looking for* snakes, not seeking to avoid them, but here are some tips in case you're in the wild with someone who doesn't share your enthusiasm, or you find yourself in dangerous snake territory and want to protect yourself. These ideas come from "Bayou Bob," who tells how to avoid sneaking up on snakes and upsetting them enough that they retaliate:

- Don't stalk along quietly, which can make a snake think it's about to become the target of a sneaky predator. Make your presence known by using good solid footsteps. The snake will sense the vibrations and get out of the way.

- Take a pet along, like a dog, since they have better antennae when it comes to snakes.

- Remember that, if you see one snake, there may be others, so be alert!

One other tip he offers. If you want to keep snakes from sneaking up and visiting you at home, put common garden-variety powdered sulfur or mothballs around your house; snakes don't like it. Don't do this if you have children or pets. Remember, too, that rainfall diminishes the effectiveness of these treatments, so you might have to reapply them.

Finally, two bits of advice about scaring away rattlesnakes. What should you do if you confront one? Nothing. Don't move, and they'll usually go away. They'd rather be heard than seen, and only bite moving targets.

Men's Journal, in March 1995, presented a second idea. In an article entitled "Venom Nation," they pointed out that:

> *A rattlesnake can strike an object up to a distance equal to half its body length. Since rattlesnakes may reach around seven feet long, if you remain just four feet away you can take photos, you can sing Pink Floyd songs, but you're unlikely to be bitten.*

Maybe you should make it a bit farther than that, and remember that snakes move. So you may have to move faster.

Are Devenomized Snakes Truly Safe?

Sometimes—but sometimes not. Why take the chance of having the operation performed? After all, if you can't be sure, and you must still treat devenomized snakes (called "venemoid") as if they have venom, why subject the snake to the procedure at all?

The reason you can't be sure the procedure works is that it's a tricky operation and isn't always successful. There have been instances in which a tiny piece of gland left behind regenerated, resulting in a hot snake. Or the snake was thought to be devenomized, but the gland had two ducts and only one was excised.

FOR LIZARD LOVERS
Try to feed your lizard food that's as close as possible to what it would get in the wild. If you feed it tropical flowers, make sure the flowers are free of insecticides.

If this happens, what are you doing to do; call a malpractice snake, ah, lawyer, eh?

Many snake owners are also against devenomization surgery for other reasons:

- It's a risky operation that can lead to complications and even death. Even if the snake survives the surgery, some venemoids won't eat afterwards, and slowly starve themselves to death.

• It's mutilation, since venom is an important part of a snake's digestive system.

• It's inhumane and unnatural to deprive an animal of its means of defense and its ability to hunt.

Those who believe it's all right to turn a perfectly healthy snake into a venemoid voice their feelings that, at the very least, the surgery should not be done to make a "safe" pet out of a snake, but to make snakes used in educational talks and shows safer for the audience.

So, if you go that route, just remember: You'll never be 100 percent certain the surgery has accomplished its goal—until it's too late.

Never Get Cocky with a Cobra

These two stories could fall into the category of "we are not amused" and serve as warning lessons to those who think they can remain in control of dangerous snakes. Even the most expert and experienced snake handlers can get a little too cocky for their own good. Perhaps too much time around venomous snakes leaves a person feeling untouchable, or maybe they just get sloppy.

Or maybe they were just idiots to begin with. Like the man who was dumb enough to place a newly hatched cobra in his mouth, showing off how the cobra's hood stood up like a little umbrella while the snake protruded from between his lips. Cute picture, huh? Not in the opinion of the cobra. Perhaps annoyed at being the butt of a silly photo op, according to *Reptiles* magazine, the snake stuck his small but deadly fangs into the lips of his owner, who had to be rushed to the hospital.

At least he survived. A second story that appeared in one of *Reptiles's* columns was in the same vein, but more dramatic. Grace Olive of Cypress, California, a collector of many venomous snakes, had a mystical power over her brood.

She sure had a way with cobras. Roy Pinney, former president of the New York Herpetological Society, and author of the *Snake Book,* said she could stroke a hissing cobra with a full, angry hood, ready to attack, and her caress would seem to gently calm the snake, which would then retract its hood and change its mind about attacking.

Sometimes she let snakes "attack" her. For example, Ms. Olive would let her king cobra repeatedly strike her palm. The trick: For a king cobra—whose venom is so powerful it has killed elephants—to get its fangs into a victim, it requires a smaller target, as in a finger. And she wasn't offering them that.

But she only had to miscalculate once. When she tried the same trick with some new snakes, a cobra somehow latched onto her middle finger and injected her with its venom.

She coolly removed the snake, put it back in its cage, and asked to have a tourniquet tied around her wrist. She collapsed shortly after this, fell into a coma, and died ninety minutes later.

We Hiss in the Shadow

In Myanmar (formerly called Burma), during an annual ceremony each year, one king cobra is presented to a particular village. When the snake rises up to its full length—which is tall enough to look someone straight in the eye—a priestess kisses it.

According to the *National Geographic* website and CD-ROM, in 1982, a priestess was bitten by an eleven-foot snake during this ceremony. Incredibly, though, she showed no signs of poisoning. She had probably developed a partial immunity to the venom, since those involved in this bizarre ceremony at least have the good sense to regularly inoculate themselves by scratching their skin with venom mixtures.

The Real Cost of Snakebites

People who have a cavalier attitude about snakebites might not be so blasé if they knew how a bite from a snake can take a big bite from their wallet.

One victim, after paying for an ambulance; emergency room; vials of antivenin; EKG; blood work; helicopter to a special hospital; cardiac care; antibiotics; plastic surgery for consultation and a simple graft; hospitalization for preoperative, operative, and post-operative care; and ambulatory surgery had a bill of about $12,000—only two-thirds of which was covered by insurance. If that seems bad, others have spent as much as $20,000—and even more.

How would you raise this kind of money fast? Hopefully not the way a Hungarian reptile catcher did after being bitten by one venomous snake. He put it in a jar and threatened to release it unless he was given the equivalent of $500, which he needed to cure the snakebite. (It's a lot cheaper there.)

> **FOR LIZARD LOVERS**
> The Komodo dragon is the heaviest lizard and has been known to eat small deer. The crocodile monitor is the longest lizard.

In addition to money, there are other costs to consider if you're unfortunate enough to receive a serious bite. There's generally a lot of pain involved in receiving and recovering from the bite, and frequently loss of some flesh, movement, and feeling in the limb that was bitten. But the ultimate price could be your life. If the bite doesn't kill you, you could die from hypersensitivity to the antivenin.

Bad enough for you?

Should You Be Afraid of Snakebites?

When people are bitten by snakes, it's said that their first question is often: "Am I going to die?"

The answer is yes—but it probably won't happen from the snakebite.

Only about 10 to 15 percent of all snakes are strongly venomous, and not all are dangerous to humans. And even if you get bitten by a bad guy, not all venom is fatal, and if your snake's is, you're unlikely to receive a fatal dose of it.

Venom is just highly evolved saliva, whose purpose is to secure food. A snake will generally not even squander it on you—since you're too big to be eaten anyway.

Snakes are not out to get you; hiding behind rocks and trees, waiting to pounce on unsuspecting passersby. When snakes attack someone, it's usually defensive, because the person has invaded their territory or frightened the snake in some way.

Although you should seek help fast if you're bitten, don't automatically panic and assume the worst. Remember, more people have died from rabies in the last half century than from snakebites. And in one year in America, more people are killed by lightning strikes than by snakebites.

Where the Bites Are, or Why Snakebite Deaths Are Higher in Certain Countries

It is said that as many as one to two million people each year are bitten by snakes; how these people fare is often not directly related to how venomous the snakes are, but in what country the bite occurs.

For example, in Australia, where they have more venomous species than nonvenomous ones—including some of the most dangerous snakes in the world—there were only four deaths in one recent year. Indeed, it is said that more people die in Australia from eating poisonous turtle meat than from being bitten by snakes.

Much of this is due to Australia's excellent program of snakebite first-aid. But that's not the only thing that determines whether people will die from a snakebite. Another is whether or not the person was wearing shoes. Many fatal snakebites occur in places like India, Pakistan, Africa, and Southeast Asia, where footwear is flimsy or people go totally bare-foot and then step on snakes, who are justifiably annoyed.

> **FOR LIZARD LOVERS**
> Don't buy lizard- or snakeskin belts, boots, hatbands, or other "fashion" products. Lizards and snakes are often skinned alive, supposedly to make the skin more supple. The poor animals may suffer for days before dying.

How good the medical facilities are—and whether people choose to go to them—are two other critical factors. Obviously bad doctors can kill good people, but even if someone is bitten in an area containing the finest medical facilities in the world, if they won't go, or can't go, for medical care, they won't be helped.

Even if the victim wants to go, if the bite occurs in a rural area, away from good medical help, it doesn't matter how modern the country's medical facilities are, or how badly the person wants to get to them. The bite victim can't get there.

Some people who can get to good medical facilities still won't go to them. They may not trust Western-style doctors and instead choose traditional doctors or some primitive treatment. Even in more modern areas, if someone refuses medical treatment, say for religious reasons, it doesn't matter how good or how available medical treatment for snakebite is.

Why Americans Usually Survive Most Snakebites

Death by venomous snakes is low in the United States; of about 8,000 venomous snakebites each year, only about a dozen kill their victims. These are some of the reasons we do better in this area than people in most countries:

- *Born to be mild:* The types of venomous snakes here generally don't kill that quickly. For example, in places like Thailand, which offers superior medical care, the Siam cobra kills so rapidly that even if there is a hospital nearby, the victim can't get there in time to be saved.

- *Land of plenty:* There are lots of hospitals that Americans can get to quickly.

- *Is there a doctor in the house?* There is good medical care at these hospitals.

- *Faith in healers, not faith healers:* People here generally believe in the medical system (even if they're annoyed at their HMOs).

- *Don't put your foot down.* Most Americans don't go around without socks and shoes in snake territory, so bites don't penetrate as deeply as bites do in "barefoot" areas.

Despite this, some experts believe that the number of deaths from snakebites is likely to rise. The increasing passion of pet owners for "hot" snakes, often purchased by people who consider pit bulls wimpy, is likely to soon haunt us.

FOR LIZARD LOVERS
When iguanas sneeze, they don't have colds. They're just sneezing salt through special glands in their nasal cavities.

The Snake Who Put the Bite on Two Americans

Gaboon vipers, whose fangs are so long they can easily cut through heavy shoes and thick clothing, are not indigenous to this country, so they rarely make the news here.

But two bites from this snake were well publicized. One snake bit a sixteen-year-old boy who was trying to steal the viper from the National Zoo in Washington. In another publicized instance when an American survived a bite from a Gaboon viper, the victim was Marlin Perkins, host of TV's *Wild Kingdom*.

The Floridian Who's Been Bitten 166 Times, or Miami on 100 Bites a Day

Almost every herper has heard of Bill Haast, founder and director of the Miami Serpentarium. Although he is now eighty-seven years old, he still goes to work each day, milking more than twenty snakes for venom that will be used by researchers and antivenin manufacturers to save lives.

Bill admits he's slowed down a bit since the days that he averaged 100 snakes a day—his all-time record was 500 in one day—at what is surely one of the world's riskiest jobs. But not only does he have the satisfaction of doing a job which saves so many lives, but venom may sell for as much as $500 an ounce.

The reason Bill has survived so many close calls is that, over the years, he has injected himself with diluted venom from over fifty different snakes. As a result, his blood is now so rich with antibodies, that it's been transfused twenty-one times into critical bite victims.

Some of his own bites have been critical. The bite of a Siamese cobra during a live broadcast of Marlin Perkins's *Zoo Parade* almost killed him. He ended up on a respirator for two days, after he stopped breathing on his own.

Another really close call came when he was bitten by what many consider to be the most dangerous snake in the world—the saw-scaled viper—before there was any antivenin for it in the United States. Some antivenin was found in Iran, and with the help of an assistant to then-president George Bush, it was raced into this country to save him.

His latest—and hopefully last—bite was from a western diamondback, and that one caused him to go into convulsions. But that still didn't stop him, because as soon as he recovered, he went back to work. Gotta admire that kind of craziness, ah, dedication.

Bill's background is as colorful as his current job. He was once a snake handler for a roadside carnival, and he also learned about snakes when he was in the moonshine business in the Everglades. When asked by this author how he felt about continually risking his life each day with his current job, he said, "I continue to do it each day because I enjoy it. I don't even think of it as risky. If you hadn't reminded me of it, I wouldn't have even thought of it."

How Antivenin Is Made

If someone is bitten, he or she must be given an antidote derived by "milking" a snake. To do this, the herpetologist holds the snake's head, while the snake bites into the rubberized covering of a container, and not into the handler. This venom, which is literally worth more than gold, is then injected into horses.

After the horse's blood becomes immune to that specific type of venom, the blood is used by people who have been bitten by that kind of snake. This is not a short process. According to *Snake Secrets,* as many as 69,000 extractions may be needed to obtain some snake antivenin.

FOR LIZARD LOVERS

To sex your lizard, put it in a clear container and look up from the underside. You can often tell a male from a female, because the males have a swollen section at the base of the tail, while the female's tail is thinner.

What to Do If You Are Bitten by a Snake, Plus Uses for Venom

A Simple Way to Get Most Snakes to Release You

Alcohol works most of the time. *On* the snake, that is, not for them. You'll have a tough time finding tiny shot glasses and ice cubes. And don't drink the alcohol when handling snakes, since it may make you more careless and more likely to get bitten.

Alcohol can also harm you after you've been bitten, because it can make the venom spread around your system more quickly, as well as making it hard for you to get your act together to seek help.

But you can toast alcohol ("Here's Looking at You, Snake") for its ability to generally get snakes to release you—most of the time. (Some experts think you should use alcohol only on bigger snakes, and only if they're past the legal drinking age.) You can mist in front of, under, over, or even on what the snake is holding on to—like your finger. (If you didn't already drink the alcohol down in a panic.)

> **FOR LIZARD LOVERS**
> Some female lizards may arch their backs and hop on stiff legs to show they don't want to mate. They may turn their heads from side to side to show they do.

Some experts say to pour alcohol right on the snake's nose, but Charles Mosher says that actually spraying the snake's head should be a last resort. "They really hate the smell of it—and there is no need to hurt them by getting it on them," he says. "Waving an open bottle usually suffices, since they hate the smell of it."

As for what type of alcohol to use, if you're around children, or abstainers, he says you may want to use 99 percent isopropanol. But most of the time, you'll do fine with any kind of drinking alcohol that's around.

If you don't have alcohol, vinegar sometimes works, and one snake owner uses small bottles of breath spray. These, he joked, have the added benefit of giving your snake nice, minty breath afterward.

Whatever you use, have it ready and close at hand if you're likely to need it. "It's not nice to have an adult ball python chewing your finger and constricting your arm while you walk around the house looking for the alcohol," says Morgan Kennedy, president-elect of the New England Herpetological Society.

What If You're Home Alone and Become "Attached" to Your Snake

If a snake is small, and the bite can't do much damage, trying to pry the snake off can hurt both of you. Hitting and punching it probably won't work, and could make the snake clench its jaws more tightly. Let the snake be, and it'll soon let you be.

If a medium snake has a grip on you, though, grasping the snake behind the jaws and pushing its head forward, toward the nose, may disengage the teeth.

What if that doesn't work? Or what if it's a *biiiigggg* snake? Dave and Tracy Barker, who raise pythons, wrote an interesting article in *The Vivarium*, describing which methods work. Based on some unhappy experiences they have had, their discouraging conclusion was that nothing works all the time.

For example, some suggest that you put the snake so rudely attached to your hand under cold water. The Barkers have tried this method and yes, the snake eventually does have to breathe—but with some snakes that could take half an hour. (And you wouldn't want to waste all that water would you?)

Holding snakes under hot water only made them bite harder. (Wouldn't you?)

Spraying stuff in their mouths didn't always work. (And could make them madder.)

Gouging their eyes wasn't always effective. (And could make them rightly furious.)

Biting their tails is, hmmm, interesting, but not necessarily efficacious. (And people would feel awfully silly afterward if that didn't work.)

Blowing air in a snake's mouth while it's biting takes nerves of steel, and may not have any payoffs (other than providing some primitive air-conditioning for the snake).

And stabbing the snake with a knife is nasty—and also often ineffective (not to mention bloody).

What to Do If You Become Your Snake's Main Squeeze

What do you do about constricting snakes? Shouting "Get a grip on yourself" isn't going to work, so is there any other way to squeeze out of a snake's grip in a pinch? Unfortunately, no.

A python's grip, for example, may be fifty times stronger than a human's. And many pythons will keep constricting—no matter what you do—until you die or quit struggling. Neither option is in your best interest. Constricting is so instinctive that snakes fed dead prey may continue to squeeze. Talk about overkill!

The one thing the Barkers thought might work—although they hadn't tried it—was a stun gun blasted across the spine of the neck region, which they thought might override the nervous system control of the snake.

How "Hot" Snakes Helped the Cold War

Since snake venom can become contaminated with radioactivity, snakes can be used for radioactivity readings to help determine contamination from nuclear waste, nuclear accidents, and nuclear explosions.

According to Steve Grenard, snake venoms (and other animal samples) were routinely checked for radioactivity levels during the Cold War, especially those in the Soviet Union, to learn the truth about nuclear activities in that country.

What Not to Do until the Doctor Comes, or Don't Do the "Movie Maneuver"

Getting bitten sucks—but don't suck your bites. Dr. Robert Norris, chief of the division of emergency medicine at Stanford University, in Palo Alto, California, warns people against doing what is so often done in movies and on TV. "When you suck venom out of a snakebite, you're also flooding the wound with oral bacteria, which can increase the chances of infection," he says.

Trying to draw in the venom with your mouth doesn't create enough suction to do that much good anyway. Furthermore, if the person doing it has sores or cuts in his or her mouth, he or she may end up in as much trouble as the bite victim.

What about tourniquets? "You'll do more harm than good by putting one on and delaying the drive to the hospital," says Norris.

Dr. Kathleen Delaney, associate professor of emergency medicine at the University of Texas Southwestern Medical Center, was quoted as saying that, instead of a tourniquet, you should tie a loose band about two inches above the bite to slow down circulation of the venom. Or if you have one, put an Ace bandage on the bite.

She also suggested that you don't hang around. Some people believe that rushing to a hospital will speed the spread of the poison through the body. Nonsense. The venom will circulate at the same rate no matter what you're doing.

Finally, don't use ice, which is a major reason why some limbs have to be amputated after a bite. "Ice increases the damage," she says.

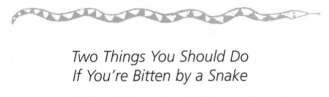

Two Things You Should Do If You're Bitten by a Snake

- Make a mental note of what the snake that bit you looks like. That could be helpful for doctors treating you.

- Get to a hospital as fast as possible. As one Vero Beach herpetologist said: "The best medicine a person has if he has been bitten by a venomous snake is his car keys." Drive to the hospital immediately—or be taken there if you can't drive.

Quacks and Snakebite "Cures"

Whether or not a hospital and orthodox Western medicine are available to treat a snakebite, many people throughout the world still choose to be treated by snake charmers. They use ancient combinations of herbs, astrology, demonology, juices of trees and leaves, snake stories, and more, while various charms are recited, masks are worn, and dances are performed. Entertaining? Yes. But many of the victims die before they can enjoy the show.

These ceremonies are based on the belief that snakes are agents of evil, and that the evil spirits that caused the bite are in the wound and must be driven away. Such a ceremony can cost as much as $200, in countries where people don't make that in a year.

If these ceremonies worked, they would be worth it, but as they said in a chilling show about cobras on the Discovery Channel, "Sometimes they are successful—but snakes don't always inject a fatal quantity of venom."

How Snake Venom Saves Lives

Snake venom contains at least twenty-six different enzymes and hundreds of proteins, and while together they can be deadly, isolated and purified, they have saved an enormous number of lives. Here is a brief summary of the work in this area; those who would like to know more about this field should read a fascinating book called *Medical Herpetology* by Steve Grenard.

- The drug Capoten, used by millions with hypertension, is based on research that was originally done with the venom of the jararacussu, after researchers realized that its bite caused a precipitous drop in the victim's blood pressure.

- Another drug, ancrod, sold under the name Arvin, and used widely in Europe for the treatment of various vascular diseases, such as deep venous thrombosis, is derived from the venom of the Malayan pit viper. Ancrod has been used to treat priapism as well.

- A product called Stypven, derived from Russell's viper venom, has helped in clotting disorders, and venom from this snake is being studied for hemophilia. In addition, other substances from snakes that affect blood clotting are also being tested for human use right now.

- Another promising area for venom is pain research. This is not surprising, since fifty years ago, cobra venom was used as an analgesic. Right now, the green mamba's venom is being used to study pain receptors in humans.

- According to the *Baltimore Sun*, Oxynor, derived from the venom of the taipan, has potential in the treatment of burns, plus as a diagnostic tool for the presence of lupus.

- Herpoxin, taken from cobra's venom, may act against replication of herpes.

• Protease inhibitor, used for AIDS, had as its basis the study of snake venom.

• Nerve growth factor, an experimental drug based on research of the venom of the spectacled cobra may help in the treatment of Parkinson's and Alzheimer's diseases.

• Since snakes are naturally enemies of rodents, snakes may also be a weapon against Lyme disease and hantavirus.

• An understanding of snakes may even help in research with epilepsy, since the hognose snake's "playing dead" is similar to some epileptic behavior.

Grenard, whose book also includes interesting information in the whole area of snakebites, says that work with snakes is also being done with emphysema, sperm motility, antibiotics, antitumor work, osteoporosis, and even colds.

Can Snake Venom Cure Cancer?

The only thing more extraordinary than some recent findings that snake venom might help cure breast cancer was the fact that this fact received so little publicity. Can you imagine how the media would have reacted if, say, some protein in cat saliva had shown even distant promise for curing some carcinomas? They would have all but interrupted the Super Bowl to trumpet the news.

This good news, ignored by almost everyone, was that, in February of 1998, researchers at the University of Southern California isolated a protein, called *contortrostatin*, from a Southern copperhead. The protein inhibits growth of cancer tumors in mice, and prevents metastasis by inhibiting adhesion of the tumor cells to the surrounding matrix.

This is not the first drug isolated from venom to prove promising with cancer. Because venom attacks tissue—as does cancer—work is or has also been done in this area using venom from the Western diamondback, the rattlesnake, and the taipan.

Heard about any of this?

Hopefully Not a Snake Oil Salesman

Although most medicinal benefits of snakes derive from the venom, one nutritionist claims that rubbing *oil* derived from Chinese water snakes into swollen joints may ease the pain of arthritis or bursitis.

Locating the snake to get the oil can be a slippery proposition, but you may be able to find some in a Chinese herb store, if this interests you.

FOR LIZARD LOVERS
Drinking water, for most lizards, must be ammonia- and chlorine-free—which means no tap water.

Slithery People and Odd Stories about Snakes

The Truth about Snake Charmers Isn't Always So Charming

Almost everything people have come to believe about snake charmers is wrong. For starters, they don't make snakes dance with their music, since snakes can't *hear* the music anyway. The snakes respond not to auditory, but to visual cues, undulating like that to follow the charmer, his pipe, or the top of the basket.

Furthermore, the snake doesn't follow the cues because it's charmed but because it wants to attack. Cobras stand erect with spread hoods when feeling threatened. They're not dancing like that because they enjoy cutting a rug. They view the flute as an enemy, following its sweeping movements in preparation to strike at it.

Finally, it isn't always as risky for the charmer as it seems. True, they use dangerous snakes, and these people don't live a charmed life. They may handle pythons or vipers, although the most common snake they use is the naja naja, one type of Asian spitting cobra—although this one doesn't spit—generally the spectacled cobra. The snake they use may be as long as twenty feet, and to amuse their audience, the charmers may dance with the snakes, kiss them, jump rope with them, and even stuff the head down their throats. Charming . . . eh?

But there are tricks many charmers use to make these snakes less deadly:

- *Some like it cold.* Some cool their snakes down before a show, which slows them down and makes them easier to handle.

- *Where's the beef?* Some overfeed their snakes, so they're sluggish and less likely to strike.

- *Fangs a lot.* Some of these snakes have had their fangs removed. Although they do grow back, this takes away the danger during the show.

- *I'm speechless.* Some snakes have had their mouths sewed up so they can't get their fangs out.

- *My bark is worse than my bite.* Some charmers use nonvenomous species.

- *The milk of human unkindness.* Some charmers milk the venom regularly to vitiate its potency.

Some charmers not only have to worry about their snakes but sometimes the law. A Nigerian snake charmer was recently charged with murder after a ten-year-old boy was accidentally attacked by his cobra during a show.

Stupid People Tricks

Khamisa, a twenty-seven-year-old snake charmer, has a mouth-watering new twist to a trade with a lot of competition. Here in the United States, snake charming is a unique profession, but in Karachi, Pakistan, where Khamisa works his odd trade, the competition is so fierce, he had to come up with something different.

Trained for a full year, Karachi, has mastered the art of snorting a live snake through his nostrils (either one will do), and then pulling it through his mouth.

The rigors of his studies have paid off financially for the creative charmer. At the end of a long day, filled with many performances of the twenty-second act, he pulls in a whopping $1.50 to $3.50.

Reverse Stories: Man Bites Snake and Snake Shoots Man

Message to snakes: Don't bite one Valentin Grimaldo. Walking along a highway in Edinburg, Texas, in May of 1997, he was bitten by a Texas coral snake, while reaching into some grass. This isn't a case of once bitten, twice shy. The snake could have used protection from Grimaldo, who bit the head off this offending creature, skinned it, and used the pelt as a tourniquet.

According to the *Beaver County Times*, a passerby took him to a nearby hospital, where he made a complete recovery.

The snake did not.

Snake Shoots Man

You know the slogan: Guns don't kill people, people kill people. Well, that may not always be the case. Sometimes it's snakes who kill people—with guns.

A few years ago, a hunter in Iran was supposedly shot to death by a snake that coiled itself around the hunter's shotgun. His friend claimed the victim was trying to catch the snake alive by pressing the butt of his shotgun behind the snake's head. But the snake instead coiled around the butt, accidentally pulling the trigger with his thrashing tail. Somehow, this fired one of the barrels and fatally shot the man in the head. This not only killed the would-be snake wrangler, but terribly embarrassed him too.

Attention Kmart Shoppers

You never know what special extras large department stores will include: Savings, red-tag sales, . . . snakes? In a Florida Kmart, according to *Florida Today*, an unfortunate shopper was bitten by an adult pigmy rattlesnake while picking up a plant.

Now, other stores are trying to get into the act. Three other people have supposedly been bitten by snakes in separate incidents in a garden center of a Wal-Mart. Do you notice a trend?

FOR LIZARD LOVERS
Heating and lighting apparatus should be covered with wire mesh, so lizards can't get near it.

The moral of the story is either to be careful in store gardening areas or that these are the place to go if you want to pick up a free snake.

Apparently, though, unexpected snake visitors don't only appear in gardening stores. Although some say these stories are urban legends, according to *News of the Weird*, a woman shopping in Wisconsin became so ill that she had to go to the emergency room of the hospital. The doctor found some scratches on her neck and, from the symptoms, concluded that she had suffered a snakebite. But how? Upon questioning, the woman recalled that while she was at the store trying on a winter coat from Taiwan, she felt a prick in her neck.

The hospital called the store, which cut the coat open. Sure enough, there was a mother and three baby snakes trapped in the lining. They had probably all crawled in to hibernate when the coat was being assembled overseas.

The woman was given a "generous" payment. (Unlike the salaries of the people who make these coats.)

Serpent Time

Believe it or not, in the dark depths of the Amazon, the largest body of fresh water on earth, there is rumored to be a snake of monstrous proportions called the *boiuna* or *cobra-grande*. That means "big cobra," and according to some eyewitness accounts this is one big, bad snake.

Believed by some to be an outsized anaconda, the boiuna is said to grow as long as sixty feet, can supposedly swallow a deer whole, and sports a head like a dinosaur with horns.

Not surprisingly, it has never been photographed. A cute picture would be one of it next to the abominable snowman, or some other mythical creature.

Attack Snakes: Using Pit Vipers Instead of Pit Bulls

Snakes As Bodyguards

You've seen the sign, "Forget the Dog, Beware of Owner," with a graphic depiction of a gun barrel pointed at your face. But a weapon is only a deterrent when someone's home to use it. What if the house is empty or the family is on vacation for an extended time?

That's where an entrepreneur in Zimbabwe comes in. According to the *New York Times*, he releases cobras into the homes of vacationing clients for

$12 a day. The house is made secure, so the cobras can't escape, and then signs are posted in two languages (plus a cartoon version for illiterate burglars) warning of the home's unusual security system.

It wouldn't work in America, where a bitten burglar would no doubt later sue the owners, the company, and probably even the snake. Furthermore, some think the whole idea of using snakes in such a manner is a new form of cruelty to animals. But others think snakes should be allowed to work and earn their keep, so they can rise above their current low station in life.

Ready, Aim, Cobra

People who wish to riot in the town of Bekasi on the outskirts of Jakarta, Indonesia, should take into account the police's new crowd-control tactic.

Dogs may be good, bullets better, but to supplement these tried-and-true methods comes cobras. According to the *Cape Argus* newspaper in South Africa, the Bekasi police plan to acquire twenty-four cobras—including king cobras—to hold in their hands to discourage rioters while facing them. What a riot!

FOR LIZARD LOVERS
Handling lizards from the time they're young generally makes them calmer when older.

Snakes That Are Not Taking a Bite Out of Crime

Here are three odd stories about criminals using snakes in unusual manners in the commission of a crime.

Blackmail by Snake

In Hungary, three men took their guns, forced a man to the ground, and injected something into his thigh, telling him to leave on his mobile phone. According to AFP news service, they called him on his cell phone a few minutes later, and informed him that they had injected deadly snake venom into his leg. They warned that it would kill him in three days until he paid $150,000 for the antidote.

Although the man was suffering from alarming symptoms such as heavy sweating and quickened heartbeat, he called the police.

This story turned out to have a sweet ending. He had been injected with insulin, not a deadly venom. He survived, and the criminals were caught.

Stick What Up?

Near Managua, Nicaragua, thieves are using poisonous snakes—actually fear of them—to rob people. It is so effective that the crooks may not even have to tie up their victims, or do anything to get them to turn over their money. One woman simply passed out when she saw the snake's fangs. The burglar then nonchalantly went through her things.

The thieves seem to be mostly after cash and jewelry, but when their victims haven't had any, they've settled for rice and beans. The news report didn't make clear whether the food was wanted for the thieves or for the snakes.

Pot Luck

In Germany, narcotics police raiding an apartment found a ten- and a thirteen-foot python guarding twenty marijuana plants. According to AFP, the police hastily retreated, after the owner told them that the pythons look for food once a month—and refused to tell them when they had last been fed.

Waiter, There's a Snake in My Soup

One con man with a big appetite but a light wallet, who also, obviously, didn't mind the taste of snake, thought he had come up with the trick to get a great meal in a restaurant— without paying for it. This rip-off artist, who lived in the Philippines, used to eat like a king, ordering everything on the menu, from soup to nuts. Then, when he got his bill, he'd slip a snake into his soup, complain, and get a free meal (and probably some bad jokes) out of the dirty deal.

One day, however, he was caught in the act. The *San Francisco Chronicle* reported that the police were called, and while he was being questioned, this buffet burglar simply ate the snake. When the police were about to take him away, he smugly asked, "Where is your evidence?"

Don't let this story give you any ideas.

Snake Smugglers and Other Stories of Cruelties Toward Snakes

Snake smuggling is big business, right up there with drugs, diamonds, and weapons. But while drugs and diamonds may be small enough to be easily hidden, many snakes are not.

Furthermore, while hard goods are usually unharmed when smuggled, many snakes are not. They may be poisoned by the sedative given to them by the traffickers, who don't care about snakes, and know they can still make money, even if a few snakes die along the way.

One final difference between inanimate contraband and snakes: the former stay quiet while being transported, while snakes may not. Two California smugglers learned this after they hid their smuggled snakes in their underwear.

These jerks thought they had it all figured out when they tied the snakes into pantyhose, tucked them in their groin area, and tried to cross the border from Mexico into Texas. They were caught when the snakes in their pants moved and the guards realized that "drugs don't move around like that." (Although sometimes people on drugs do.)

FOR LIZARD LOVERS

If you've having trouble cutting your lizard's nails because they're too brittle, try increasing the frequency of its baths, suggests Melissa Kaplan, who maintains the largest (and best) lizard site on the Internet. Cut your lizard's nails while they're still damp, and it'll be easier.

Wouldn't Hurt a Fly—a Python, on the Other Hand . . .

Examples of cruelty toward wild snakes are legion, and some idiots are even cruel to their own snakes. A few years ago, in Birmingham, England, a twenty-year-old reptile keeper was fined and banned from keeping animals for ten years after admitting to subjecting a ball python to unnecessary suffering.

According to the *Express Star*, this bum allowed the python to burn against a bare lightbulb, and the pain and shock led to the snake's refusal to eat, and ultimately to its death.

In another case, a thirty-nine-year-old man from Yorkshire, England, was found guilty of starving his thirteen-foot Burmese python to death, and probably trampling on it as well.

Thankfully, this Yorkshire terrorist will never have the opportunity to harm another animal, since he was not only fined but banned from keeping reptiles for life. It's unlikely that American courts would have punished the offenders as severely, or even treated the cases seriously.

"He was cruel to a *what?* Next case please."

SNAKE BITES
Snakes can get leukemia and cancer.

World's Weirdest Snake Story

This is not made up, folks. In 1973, a forty-two-year-old man in China claimed to have eaten 10,000 *live* snakes in the previous two decades. Why he ate them is unknown—perhaps he thought a snake a day would keep the doctor away—but he said he "felt miserable" if he didn't have at least one each day.

Is this man happy? According to *USA Today*, no, because no one will marry this snake eater. Perhaps because dating is a bit of a problem. "You can see how [he] gets into trouble after he lines up a dinner date. The obvious question—'What'll we have?'—must lead to some real conversation stoppers."

FOR LIZARD LOVERS

Some think side doors are better than top openings in a lizard habitat, since reaching in to pick up a lizard may scare it. Many predators (like birds) approach their prey from above, so coming in toward your lizard at the same angle may trigger its fear instinct. Let the lizard be above you when you free it, so you must reach up to do so.

Snakes for Dummies, or What You May Not Know about Snakes

Questions Often Asked Lawyers about Pet Snakes, or the Scales of Justice

What do people ask lawyers about snakes? I asked Taryn L. Hook-Merdes—one of America's most famous lawyers specializing in reptiles—who is the co-founder and former president of the Fairbanks Herpetological Society, a freelance writer, law professor, and attorney licensed to practice in Alaska (her home base), California, and New York.

She also currently owns a Dumeril's ground boa constrictor, and "snake-sits" for a nine-foot Burmese python, a California king snake, and a six-foot boa. Here are questions she's commonly asked and her answers.

If my snake hurts someone, will I have to pay damages? Generally, yes, and you may also be responsible for medical expenses, pain and suffering, lost wages, and more.

What damages will I have to pay if my snake eats my neighbor's pet? You will normally be responsible for the "value" of the animal. For example, in one case, a seven-foot boa constrictor slithered out his owner's window and ate a neighbor's two-pound Chihuahua. It was an accident, but the owner was ordered to pay $1,500 for the value of the Chihuahua. The dog's owner originally asked for $5,000.

But what if my snake is tame? Your "domesticated" snake may be as docile as a puppy or as cuddly as a pussycat, but traditional personal injury laws still consider it a wild animal. In one case, two Burmese pythons (fifteen to twenty feet long) were so tame they regularly swam with children at pool parties. Nevertheless, they were deemed undomesticated dangerous animals.

> **FOR LIZARD LOVERS**
> If you have trouble restraining your lizard to clip its nails, wrap it in a large towel, pull out one claw at a time, and clip away.

Are personal injury laws the same for snakes as they are for domesticated pets, such as cats and dogs? No, they're usually stricter. Even if you acted responsibly, you may have to get out your checkbook if something happens.

For example, suppose you placed your snake in a secure, locked cage with "DANGER" signs in place. A neighbor's child breaks open the lock and is severely bitten. You are still responsible for damages.

What if a trespasser is bitten by my snake? A few older cases hold that trespassers can sue you if your wild animal hurts them.

I want a large constrictor. Are there any special laws? Yes, some jurisdictions require special permits for large snake ownership, and some ban certain snakes outright. Speak to an attorney.

Does my personal injury insurance policy cover damage caused by my snake? Call your local insurance agent to review your existing policies, including general liability, homeowners, umbrellas, and rental. Ask if snakes are covered—and for what. If they're not, ask about an "endorsement" or extra policy to cover snakes.

What other things can I do to protect myself? Provide your snake with a secure cage, including a sturdy top and lock. If guests handle your snake, supervise them. Make sure they wash their hands with antibacterial soap afterward. Never display or allow anyone to touch sick or aggressive snakes, snakes with parasites or ticks, or snakes preparing to shed.

> **FOR LIZARD LOVERS**
> Don't put driftwood in the habitat, since it may have been sitting in water for a long time and be rotten inside. Also, don't use cedar or pine branches. Cedar bedding can be harmful to many lizards.

Consult your veterinarian about other medical issues.

Can I take my snake with me on an airplane? Each airline has its own travel regulations concerning reptiles; those that do permit them insist on snakes traveling in the cargo hold. If you're traveling overseas, many foreign countries have strict quarantine and admissions standards for exotic animals. Contact the appropriate embassy or consulate for specific information.

I saw a nice-looking snake in the park. Can I adopt it as a pet? No. Do not collect pets in the wild—even in your own backyard. Many states zealously guard certain types of snakes, because they are endangered or threatened. If you take one as a pet without a permit—even the most common-looking snake—you could face criminal penalties and fines.

What if I buy a snake at a pet store and it is sick or dies? Can I get my money back or a new snake? It depends on the purchase/sale contract. Usually, the fine print includes a very short warranty period, such as forty-eight hours. During that time, most stores will replace your pet or give you money back if it gets sick.

Seventeen Interesting Facts You May Not Know about Snakes

1. *Slippery creatures.* Snakes can't move on a totally smooth surface, such as glass, because their belly scales need to catch and hold on to key points on the ground or on the branches of a tree.

2. *Sneezed to meet ya.* Sea snakes have nostrils on top of their heads.

3. *What did you say?* Snake's ancestors probably lost their ears to help them burrow more easily.

4. *Come on in, the water's fine.* Almost all snakes can swim.

5. *Snakes preserve us!* Pythons and boas are the most ancient of modern snakes.

6. *Spurs them on.* Pythons, boas, and anacondas have two tiny vestigial back legs, called *spurs*, which remain from their lizard backgrounds.

> FOR LIZARD LOVERS
> A chameleon's tongue may be as long as the lizard itself.

7. *It's what's up front that counts.* No snakes even have traces of front limbs.

8. *Baby, it's dark outside.* Many snakes change color according to the temperature; for example, becoming darker when it is colder.

9. *Horny.* A few breeds of snakes, like the horned puff adder, have, yep, horns. Horns on desert snakes probably help keep sand off their eyeballs while they're resting.

10. *Old pink eyes.* An albino snake has pink eyes.

11. *You can bank on this.* According to the *Bulletin of the Chicago Herpetological Society*, 483 coins throughout the world contain images of snakes.

12. *Hail to the . . . snake?* One snake is considered to be a national monument. The albino rat snake, in Japan, is protected by the Japanese government.

13. Some snakes never leave the sea and give birth to live, fully formed young in the ocean.

14. Snakes have no bladders. Their urine is solid and excreted with their feces.

15. Snakes continue to grow throughout their lifetimes, so a large snake of a particular species is always old.

16. Snakes are more closely related to birds than to turtles—and even more closely related to dinosaurs than birds—which is just one of the many interesting facts about snakes in Harry W. Greene's *Snakes: Evolution of Mystery in Nature.*

17. Snakes can get cataracts.

Swimming Right Along (Sea Snakes)

You thought *Jaws* made you afraid to go into the water? Listen to this: Swimming in the warmer waters of the sea are approximately fifty-five types of sea snakes—including some of the world's most venomous snakes. And these terrifying sea snakes, which can breathe air and stay submerged for up to two hours, aren't tiny little minnows. Some of them grow as long as ten feet!

Sea snakes are generally found (or avoided) in warmer, shallower water—where there is no strong surf or current—and on coral reefs, where several hundred may congregate to mate.

Not only divers have to worry about them. Fishermen have run into serious problems when sea snakes become entangled in their nets. Fortunately, sea snakes rarely bite people, usually fleeing instead, probably a wise move for all sentient creatures.

Furthermore, when they do bite, the bite's often not that deep—especially if the person is wearing scuba gear. One danger is that victims may not even be aware that they've been bitten and can become unconscious and die from the bite while still underwater, which is always unsettling.

You're Wrong If You Believe This about Snakes

1. Most snakes are harmful.

   False: Most snakes are harmless.

2. Snakes can't smell with their noses.

   False: They smell with their noses, but the tongue and Jacobson's organ (an indentation on the roof of their mouth with many nerve endings) are more important to them.

3. Snakes feel slimy.

   False: Touch one. It's usually warm and dry.

4. The purpose of scales is to keep snakes warm.

   False: Scales are watertight. The main purpose is to keep moisture in, so the snake won't dry out in the heat.

5. Snakes can hypnotize people and animals.

   False: The myth probably arose because of the way snakes stare without moving, and many animals freeze when a snake stares at them. (As do many people.)

6. Snake scales are heavy.

   False: They're actually as thin as paper.

7. Snakes are cold.

   False: Some snakes can maintain body temperatures of over 100 degrees—higher than humans (who can create their own body heat).

8. Snakes are aggressive and strike whenever possible.

   False: Most snakes are cowards that prefer to swish away and avoid a fight.

9. Snakes don't have backbones.

   False: Snakes sometimes have as many as 300 vertebrae—compared to a person who has only 33 or 34.

Moving Right Along, or Can Snakes Moon Walk?

Well, not exactly, but while most people think of snakes as only slithering along the ground, some have other moves in their repertoires as well.

- Snakes like the African burrowing snake can move backward as easily as forward.

- Several desert species move sideways, by making a coil in their bodies and then throwing themselves across the ground, called "sidewinding." (This can lead to mysterious marks in the sand that might show up in a future *X-Files* episode. "Scully, we got another report of a snake abduction in the desert.")

- Sea snakes not only swim in the traditional way but can often swim backward as well. (But they probably can't do the side-stroke, breast stroke, or doggy paddle.)

- Some snakes, like a jumping viper, can leap as high as three feet in the air.

- The flying snake, which can be as long as five feet, doesn't fly, but it looks like it is as it glides smoothly through the air, changing its shape so that its body acts like a parachute. (And if you listen carefully, you may hear a "Geronimo"-like hiss emanating from its scaly lips.)

What Snakes Can See, Smell, Hear, and "Say"

What snakes can see: Most snakes don't see well, at least by people standards. They can't see in total darkness, but many can still feel the warmth of a nearby animal, through holes in their heads, called *pits*. (Telling these snakes that they have "holes in their head" is not an insult.)

What snakes can smell: Since they don't see well, snakes must depend upon their far-better-developed sense of smell to locate prey and sexual partners. Some can even use this sensitive equipment to smell water at a distance.

Snakes use their tongue for smell, tasting the world, and identifying potential prey or threats from the chemicals picked up in the air. The fork in the tongue is like a direction finder, helping a snake determine if the odor

FOR LIZARD LOVERS
If you want an exotic, rainforest effect, you can buy a humidifier that is placed in a water bowl, which makes a white "smoke" rise out of the water.

is coming from the right- or left-hand side. So if someone ever says that you "speak with a forked tongue," just say, "The better to smell you with" and totally confuse them.

Once a snake finds something in the air, or on the ground, with its tongue—which it can stick out even when its mouth is closed—it puts its tongue back in its little head and flicks it around the inside of its mouth. This transfers the chemicals to the Jacobson's organ, a region of chemically sensitive nerve ending in the roof of the mouth that functions like a cross between the senses of taste and smell.

What snakes can hear: Hear Ye. Hear Ye. Are snakes really deaf? Well, they don't have external or middle ear structures the way people do, and can't "hear" a human voice the way we can. But they do have inner ear structures that can feel sound vibrations in the ground, and they can hear low-frequency sounds, basically through their jawbones.

When sound comes through the air, the waves are absorbed by the snake's skin—snakes sort of listen through their bellies—and this is transferred to, of all places, their lungs, before traveling to a nerve that goes to the brain.

Here's Staring at You Kid, or Where the Heck Are Their Eyelids?

Many people think snakes don't have eyelids, since snakes don't blink and have that well-known glassy stare. But snakes *do* have eyelids; they're just fused shut, and they can see through them.

These eyelids are a thin transparent covering, often compared to the glass that covers a wristwatch. These "spectacles" are shed when a snake sloughs off its skin, so the only time a snake's eyelids can be seen is when they're not "wearing" them.

FOR LIZARD LOVERS
If you're putting plants in your lizard's cage, plant at an angle within the pots or in the ground, so the trunks are more natural looking.

Snake, Rattle, and Moan

Generally, no noise is good noise, when it comes to snakes. Not all of them hiss, but the majority do have *some* sound, such as a popping or bubbling, that serves as a warning to those who come near. Oddly enough, some species lift their tails and emit sounds from there when an enemy approaches, almost a reptilian version of warning by flatulence.

Of course the most famous sound a snake makes is the notorious rattle. Although most snakes twitch their tails when aroused, only the rattlesnake's tail vibration is loud and distinctive enough to have become famous.

Some snake sounds are extremely unusual. Heart-stopping king cobras, for example, are known to have a very weird moan. Cobras also hiss, which is said to sound more like a dog's growl. If you want to check this out for yourself, you can listen to it on the National Geographic website, www.nationalgeographic.com.

(For other snake-related websites, please see pages 172-173.)

Strange Ways Snakes Protect Themselves

Could have fooled him. Some snakes confound their enemies by pretending to be more dangerous than they are. For example, the harmless milk snake has the same skin coloring as the deadly coral snake. (That works well until they come into contact with a real coral snake, who doesn't think it's at all funny.)

Don't let them rattle you. Some snakes confuse their enemies by sounding more dangerous than they are. Harmless blue racers and corn snakes "buzz," or vibrate their tails rapidly back and forth when under stress, scaring off possible predators by sounding like rattlesnakes to those who don't know better.

> **FOR LIZARD LOVERS**
> When buying plants, choose those with strong and sturdy leaves and stems, so they can hold the animal's weight.

A snake in the tree. In the jungle, snakes may camouflage themselves as green vines, even hanging from branches. Watch out, Tarzan!

Don't give me any of that lip. Some snakes raise their upper lips like a snarling dog when they're threatened, scaring others away with their exposed gums and the inside of their lips.

A few other odd ways snakes intimidate enemies, according to researchers like Chris Mattison:

- Puffing up their bodies

- Bleeding from their orifices (sort of a snake stigmata)

- Rolling into a ball and hiding their heads

- Spreading a hood (sort of like *Little Red Riding Snake*)

- Ejecting disgusting or dangerous substances

- Startling the attacker with bright or distinctive markings

- Making strange sounds (kind of like today's rock groups)

- Making believe their tail is their head (thereby protecting their heads)

What a Stink!

Your nose knows when you run a-foul of a stink snake, because when they're frightened, they raise their tails and make a rotten smell that hangs around the air for a long time. They don't call them stink snakes for nothing.

But they're not the only snakes that defend themselves by stinking up the place. According to Mattison in *Snakes of the World*, many snakes defecate copiously when molested, and some even have a particularly smelly concoction that they try to smear over their attackers. It's believed that these work because predators may be put off, thinking: "If a snake smells this bad, it must taste even worse."

Playing Dead

Some snakes make believe they're dead when threatened. For example, the twig snake will lie totally still, looking like a you-know-what. But some snakes go much farther than that, and *really* play dead.

When an enemy appears, the North American hognose will usually first try to scare it off by puffing up and hissing. But if this doesn't discourage the intruder, the hognose appears to go into convulsions: lying on its back, becoming limp, and letting its tongue hang out. Since most animals prefer their meals fresh, the potential predator generally goes off in search of what it thinks is a livelier meal.

Goodbye Guam—Aloha Hawaii

There goes the neighborhood. In Guam, the brown tree snake—which bears an uncanny resemblance to James Carvill, the man best known for being Bill Clinton's pit bull-henchman—has become a serious problem. Guam has become overrun with a plague-like infestation of these BTSs, suffering with as many as 12,000 brown snakes per square mile. Since the snake has no natural predator, brown tree snakes continue to reproduce unchecked.

The snakes are close to extinguishing Guam's indigenous bird life; they eat small farm animals; and they've accidentally cut power by climbing on cables. Worst of all, these snakes, which can grow to nine feet and even longer, have bitten newborns, mistaking them for food. Nice, eh? If they ever come to this country, they can duke it out with the killer bees.

FOR LIZARD LOVERS

Many lizards bob their heads more during the breeding season. Iguana head bobbing is usually a way to say that they're the boss.

Their first stop is likely to be Hawaii. Because of Honolulu's isolation and association with Guam, it is vulnerable to the same invasion of brown tree snakes as Guam. So far, Hawaii has had almost no snakes there outside of those housed in zoos. And they want to keep it that way.

So you can imagine how upset they were in Honolulu that this same aggressive, venomous predator ruining Guam has been seen sneaking off military air transports from that beleaguered country.

So far, at least six Guam-based snakes have been found—and killed. Hawaii is so nervous about this that, according to the *Washington Post*, anyone caught with a snake in Hawaii faces a year in jail and a maximum fine of $25,000.

So Mr. and Mrs. snake owner, if you want to take your snake on vacation, avoid the Hawaiian Isles—unless you want to get a nice Hawaiian punch from the authorities.

How Three Species of Snakes Were Given the Wrong Names, or You Can't Judge a Snake by Its Cover

Corn snakes do not like their corn creamed or on the cob. And when milk snakes lose weight, they do not produce skim milk. These two snakes have no direct connection to what they were named for.

Milk Snakes

Milk snakes got their name because of the erroneous belief that they milked cows, or latched onto a cow and drank it dry. This old wives' tale probably got started because milk snakes were often found in barns—after all, that's where the rodents are—and people thought the snakes went there because they found cows to be udder-ly irresistible.

Corn Snakes

Corn snakes got their name because farmers thought the snakes were eating their corn, this time because the snakes hung around the cornfield, where the mice that ate the corn lived.

King Snakes

King snakes were not named because of any relation to Elvis, or any real royalty, but because they were thought to be kings of the jungle. This was posited on their ability to overpower and eat nearly any other snake, even venomous ones like rattlesnakes.

So what's in a name? With snakes, not always much.

> **FOR LIZARD LOVERS**
> Adult male iguanas can be very aggressive during breeding season—sometimes toward a female owner—so watch out.

Don't Get Rattled! Interesting Information about America's Most Famous Snake

When the average American thinks snake, he or she thinks rattler. Knowing a bit about these notorious animals may make you less, well, rattled, if you should encounter one.

Here are some interesting facts about them, some from the *Beastly Book* and some from snake expert Allan Puskar in an article in *Reptiles* magazine on the timber rattlesnake:

- There are more than two dozen species of rattlesnakes.
- The bite of a baby rattler can be fatal.
- A baby rattler doesn't rattle, since the sound is produced by the shedding of skin. Since an infant has only shed once, it only has one segment.
- Each progressive shedding creates another segment of the rattler's rattle.
- The more segments, the louder the rattle.
- Most rattlesnakes don't even have ten rattles.
- The louder the rattle, the bigger the snake, since a segment is added each time the snake sheds its skin.
- Some people believe you can determine the age of a rattler from the number of segments on its tail. You can't. That just shows you how many times the snake has shed, and even this is not always accurate, as rattles can wear out and break off, independently of whether a snake sheds.
- There's nothing inside the snake's rattler to give it that sound; it's just the banging of several loose, interlocking segments of what's basically dead skin.
- The sound of a rattler can be heard 100 feet away.
- The rattlesnake can't hear its own rattle.
- The rattle is more like the sound of hissing steam than a true rattling sound.
- The rattle is made of keratin, like a human fingernail.

- The oldest living rattler was a timber rattlesnake that lived more than thirty-six years.

- A rattler has extremely good eyesight. Even at what is usually a safe distance of sixteen feet, a rattler can see you, get nervous, and begin to shake its tail anxiously. But snakes usually rely not on sight but on vibrations—which they can feel from a long way off—that tell them that you are approaching.

- Once a rattler has gotten its fangs into nonhuman prey, it's generally all over for the victim. The snake will bite a small mammal, release it, and then follow the scent trail of the wounded animal and finish it off.

- Rattlers can't track birds, which can fly away, so the snakes swallow birds where they catch them.

- Rattlesnakes kill more people in America than any other snake—but still not that many. About 8,000 people are bitten each year in the United States by rattlers, and about ten to fifteen people each year die from them.

Shocking Snake Behavior

Zoologist Theodore Vonstille, of the Envi-Sci Center in Winter Park, Florida, believes that rattlesnakes emit electricity that helps them find food. Presenting his theory in *New Science*, he said that all snakes gather static electricity when they crawl. Rattlers may then release this built-up charge through their rattler as an "electrosense." This charge locates pockets of moist air that could emanate from a prey's breath or shelter.

How? The air packs an electric charge that the snake can then detect with its tongue.

Rattlesnakes got all the juice.

Amazing Records, Unusual Snakes

- There are 2,500 to 3,000 different kinds of snakes (probably a figure somewhere between, but who's counting?).

- The fastest snake is the black mamba, which some say can go twelve miles per hour, faster than people can jog. (Unfortunately, this is one of the snakes known to chase people.)

- The snake with the longest fangs is a Gaboon viper.

- The world's smallest snakes are thread or bootlace snakes and blind snakes. Some are only a few inches long, and it's said they could crawl through a pencil if you removed the lead.

- The longest-living snake may have been a zoo-dwelling boa constrictor called Popeye, who died at over forty, according to the book *I Didn't Know That Some Snakes Spit Poison*. But others say the oldest snake was a ball python who died at the age of 47¹/2 in the Philadelphia Zoo.

- The longest snake is most likely the reticulated python, and the largest measured was 32 feet, 9¹/2 inches, weighing 330 pounds, according to the *Guinness Book of Records*.

- Most agree that the greatest authenticated length and weight recorded for an anaconda was a 27-foot, 9-inch green anaconda killed in Brazil in 1960, which had a girth of 44 inches and weighed 500 pounds, according to Roy Pinney, columnist for *Reptiles*.

- Others claim that the longest was a green anaconda shot in 1944 that measured 37¹/2 feet, but that record has been disputed, since it was based on a skin, which may have been stretched.

SNAKE BITES
Killing people with snakes
was a method of execution
in ancient times.

• The largest pet snake, according to *Guinness Book of Pet Records*, was a female python named Cassius, measuring 25 feet 6 inches and weighing 240 pounds when she died in 1980.

• According to herpetologist Alan Moss, the "stinkiest snake" prize goes to *Elaphe quadrivirgate* or *Elaphe carinata*. "After catching one, no amount of washing with soap removes the smell, for about a day."

• According to the *Herpetological Review*, the longest rattle string was thirty-eight rattles. Long rattle strings are rare, and only likely to happen in captive species, since wild rattlesnakes are more likely to have their rattlers damaged.

Why There's Disagreement over Records

There are a lot of arguments about records because people often rely on anecdotal reports. Who wants to get close enough to check a giant snake out, even if one had the opportunity?

In addition, people are often so excited when they see a large snake (in some cases, *any* snake) that they don't remember what they saw afterwards. Additionally, some measurements of size have been based on stretched skins, which are not the same as the actual size of the snake.

And finally, let's face it: Some people do exaggerate. If you think people stretch the truth a bit about the size of the *fish* they caught, you ought to hear what some of them have to say about the size of the snake they encountered.

FOR LIZARD LOVERS
When buying a lizard, a captive breed is generally healthier, cheaper, less delicate, more likely to live, and more likely to take its food dead or frozen, according to *Yankee* magazine's "Practical Pet Solutions."

The World's Rarest Snake

Only about fifty-five specimens are known to exist of the Antiguan racer, found on the Great Bird Island, off Antigua. After they almost became extinct, surgically implanted electronic tags were used to find out why the young ones were being killed and the old ones were being injured.

It turned out that black rats were jumping off cargo ships, swimming to the island, attacking the snakes, and eating their eggs, according to England's *Sunday Observer*. The rats were then wiped out with poison, and the Antiguan racer—which can grow to more than two feet—is now thriving on this Caribbean island again.

World's Most Unusual Record

Here's an unusual record, although the *Kingston Whig-Standard*, which reported this story, never explained why anyone would want to capture it. Nonetheless, at the end of 1995, a twenty-five-year-old Chinese woman set a world record for living with the most venomous snakes.

To acquire this dubious honor, she spent twelve days whooping it up in a room containing 888 venomous snakes, 666 of which were cobras. Some of the others were nonvenomous, and possibly placed there for the

FOR LIZARD LOVERS
If you're trying to breed two lizards and nothing happens, next time try taking the female out of the male's enclosure for a week before the breeding season and then reintroduce them.

delectation of the cobras. These were then replaced with live snakes so as not to reduce the number of snakes in the room.

The previous record was set by a Singaporean who lived with 200 snakes for ten days. Again, no one knows why or seems to be anxious to find out, but you can bet on some loon trying to break that record.

Incidentally, you may have seen the AP report last year that some idiot in Thailand did indeed try to break that record, and apparently thought he succeeded after spending *only* one week in a glass-walled room in a shopping center with *only* 100 cobras—and ordinary ones at that, except for two kings. What a coward; just ignore him.

A Two-Headed Snake

Are two heads better than one? Sometimes. In Sri Lanka they're usually not that thrilled to find one more Russell's viper, since they're the main cause of snakebite deaths in that country. But they were very excited when they found a two-headed specimen—with four eyes, two brains, two tongues, two noses, and two esophagi—because of its potential to attract tourists.

APF, which first reported this story, wrote that before this freak snake could be seen by many people, it died at the age of three months. Although two-headed snakes have been known to fight over food, this appeared to be a natural death, and not a weird case of sibling rivalry.

On the plus side, at least the zoo won't have to answer a lot of dumb questions like:

"How do you feed a two-headed snake?"

"Eh, twice."

The Lost Snake

What was that snake in *The Lost World: Jurassic Park*? Snake expert, writer, photographer, lecturer, etc., Bill Love believes the real snake amid all the fake prehistoric reptiles was a Pueblan milk snake, a nocturnal and secretive Mexican snake.

How realistically was it portrayed? "I'd always considered it to be totally harmless, until I saw how it scared the character in the film so badly that he ran out of the cave into the jaws of the Tyrannosaurus," he wrote in *Reptiles*, where he is a regular columnist.

What Snakes Think—and What Do They Think of You?

Does it mean anything if your snake ignores you, mopes around its tank all day, never sheds, and hardly ever touches its mouse? Would it like you more if you fed it only the best organically farmed rodents and sparkling water from the Alps, and if it lived in a vivarium you had had designed by a team of prominent architects?

Unfortunately, there's not too much you can do to strengthen the snake-person bond. Since humans and snakes have never been too buddy buddy to begin with, it wouldn't be natural for them to like us all that much, or go out of their way to seek our companionship.

But just because snakes have no interest in becoming our best friends doesn't mean that some can't come to enjoy our company—and our hands. In general, snakes have a lot of tactile receptors, making some receptive to being touched. Some snakes even develop a taste for being handled; for example, enjoying having their neck scratched. Of course some cynics insist that's just because their neck *itches*, and they have no arms to scratch it.

But many people feel snakes derive actual pleasure in our companionship, beyond being scratched or obtaining pleasurable warmth from our bodies. Says Cynthia Merritt of Nashville, Tennessee, who keeps twenty-six snakes:

> *I have a four-year-old female CalKing who exhibits signs of truly liking to be handled. Sometimes at feeding time, she will get excited as I approach her cage. She will push the mouse away, coil around my arm, and travel up my shoulder, where she perches for about a half hour.*

Such stories are not that uncommon. Michelle Mavity's ball python likes to be cuddled a bit before being put back in its tank for a nap. She discovered this after letting it soak, and seeing that it would then wrap itself tightly around her arm and snuggle back into its towel. "When it was done cuddling, it slithered out of the towel and wrapped around my arm again," she recalls.

Some snakes also react badly when their owners go away. One herper, who left his snakes in the care of his brothers, found his snake seemed angry with him when he returned. The snake would hiss at him, sounding like a punctured tire when he went to handle it. Fortunately the snake got over it in a week.

FOR LIZARD LOVERS
If you're putting a pile of rocks in a lizard's habitat, cement the rocks together and always leave a few hiding places.

Many snakes who are friendly toward certain people have been handled a lot, usually by them. Indeed, it is possible that if the handling stops, it may change a snake's personality. Reticulated pythons have a reputation for being nasty when older but friendly as babies, and some people say that's because the snakes are handled less when they get large.

These are all examples of snakes acting "affectionately," but it's still a far cry from a snake's being friendly to one, being loving, the way, say, a dog loves its owner. But snakes can't give "love" since such emotions are produced in the cerebral cortex, which is undeveloped in snakes.

Then what are they giving and what are they accepting? Someone called "Lizard Loft," on the Internet, says that snakes are really "vibe" animals. This person says that snakes are attuned to our vibrations—whether love or fear—and when we "throw out swelled up love as it cuddles, it's a good vibe which instinctively is a calming force on the snake."

The snake may come to like this and, by association, the person responsible. As snake owner Zigi Blum, of Eugene, Oregon, says:

> If a particular snake finds the scent of its human non-threatening, the warmth pleasant, and maybe their caresses to be positive stimuli, it's not out of line or out of possibility to say the snake "likes" it.

The opposite probably also holds true, perhaps explaining why snakes don't like certain people. They may be turned off by muscle tension and nervous motions, especially since such actions may be exhibited by predators sizing them up in the wild. The snakes simply get bad vibes from it.

So, the bottom line here appears to be that some snakes seem to like some people under some circumstances. But don't expect yours to send you a Valentine's Day card.

FOR LIZARD LOVERS
Some lizards have many clutches of eggs throughout their lives, even though they've only mated once.

Do Snakes Have Feelings?

Snakes have no emotions as we know them; for example, they're not real happy to hear from an old snake friend, and cupid's bow (boa?) and arrow rarely, if ever, strikes them.

But just because they don't become elated, or fall in love, doesn't mean they don't have primitive "feelings." The hypothalamus is the part of the brain where most of our emotions come from, and since snakes have a hypothalamus, maybe they have a soft and romantic side we don't know about. Well, probably not.

But they do experience the most basic emotions, like fear, aggression, and pleasure. We can see that snakes avoid what they fear, attack what makes them angry, and seek out what is pleasurable. Don't we all?

How to Tell If a Snake Likes to Be Petted

Don't rub a snake the wrong way! Very few snakes like to be petted—especially on the head—the way a dog or cat does. But once in a while, some of them do get used to it, even developing a taste for it, and show obvious signs of sincerely enjoying it.

Here is how one person claims anyone can tell if a snake really enjoys being petted (or is just putting up with it so as not to hurt your feelings):

- They don't run away given the option.

- They don't try to avoid your touch.

- They stay around, even if you stop.

- They go to sleep in your arms.

- They don't hiss.

- They don't bite you.

Ten Ways to Get a Snake to "Like" You More

Although a snake is never going to lick your face like a dog or rub its tail against your leg like a cat, it *is* possible to do certain things that over time will get your snake to "like" you more.

1. Handling—especially when young—does make some snakes, well, cuddlier. Dave Karmann, a naturalist educator at the Trailside Nature Museum in New York, found when he taught at an all-girl's school and each snake was assured of at least one hour of being held each school day, after weeks and months of being caressed by a roomful of thirteen- to seventeen-year-old girls, this "mellowed out the most reluctant of my fellows." (Of course, regularly being cuddled by young girls would probably mellow out *any* fellow, not just the no-legged kind.)

2. Holding a snake close to your body may help get it to like you more. Karmann sometimes puts his small snakes in his tucked and belted shirt pockets, and leaves them there for hours. "After a while, in this dark and cozy place, they get used to the feel and smell of the person and it helps." Not to mention deterring any pickpockets!

FOR LIZARD LOVERS
When chameleons court, the female carries the male around on her back.

3. The younger your snakes are when you start handling and holding them, especially if you start when they are hatchlings, the better off you may be later. (Caressing eggs *prior* to hatch won't make any difference.)

4. Buy captive-born rather than wild-born snakes, since the latter may think anyone handling them—or even noticing them—is preparing to eat them.

5. Be as calm as possible whenever you handle your snake. The owner of ten pythons and five boas says, "I use the 'no fear' approach. The snakes can sense it if I'm afraid, and if I act like I'm not afraid, they relax much quicker."

6. Restrain yourself from restraining them. As one person admitted, "If I ever restrain them, they immediately go nuts. When they are gently supported, they are much easier to calm down."

7. Don't yank snakes. They don't like it. (Would you?) Touch them carefully. (You can yank a doodle dandy, but don't yank a snake.)

8. Occasionally keep the habitat temperature at the low end, maybe lowering it two to four degrees, so that when you pick the snake up, you're a treat. This is what Charles Mosher, who always has good ideas about snakes, calls a "dirty trick," and he suggested the next two as well.

9. Create a "dining room"–like atmosphere for your snake to eat in, and only give it food when its mood is right. In other words, take the snake out and feed it in a separate container—but not if it's acting surly. If it is, keep it in its "bedroom" and try again later. (One joker points out that admonishments are probably useless. "No dessert for you until you realize what a bad bad snake you've been.")

10. Handle snakes at times that are right for them, says Mosher. Boids, for example, are nocturnal snakes, so to calm them down, and get them closer to you, you should handle and feed them at night.

Is There Such a Thing As a "Lap" Snake?

Snakes who like to curl in your lap or be held may not be reacting emotionally. They may simply like to be where it's warm, and a human body, especially a lap, is a warm place to curl up.

But for whatever reason, some snakes do like to sit on, or stay with, or be close to their owners. "My ball python is the closest thing to a lap snake I've seen," says Frank Gould, a licensed wildlife rehabilitator and owner of Reptile Rescue and Rehab, in Towson, Maryland. "It's calm and willing to tolerate being handled."

Says another of his snake: "Once mine calms down and finds a comfy spot on my lap, it will stay there for hours." And says a third: "It's usually pretty happy sitting on us, or near us. Or else it's trying to climb the lamp."

Do Snakes Like Each Other, or Why Don't You Slither Up and See Me Some Time?

There are no snake personal ads, no hands to hold, or candlelight dinners for wild snakes. Since snakes do not form communities in the wild, nor are they territorial like dogs, don't expect them to boogie when they're captive and forced to live together. Most snakes don't seek each other out, and don't show affection toward each other the way, say, mammals do.

Still, some snakes do congregate together, like timber rattlesnakes, who can sometimes be found in colonies with fifteen to twenty snakes in them. Snakes in groups may bask together, insulate each other, huddle together, breed, hibernate, and share hiding areas. In fact, it has been found among some snakes that "even if they have ample locations to choose from, they seem to choose to be together," says Dave Karmann of the Trailside Nature Museum.

The problem is they don't appear to have much to do with each other when they *do* get together. Some snakes are downright hostile to each other, and would just as soon eat a fellow snake as look at it. (Not that many warm-blooded creatures couldn't relate to that at times.)

Indeed, many snakes don't even want to look at other snakes and become upset or stressed when in their presence. (Again, snakes may not be that different from people.) Some steal food from each other, and in a hunting frenzy, accidentally grab each other. Many snakes, when communally housed, stop feeding altogether. Once removed to individual containers, feeding behavior starts again.

So what's the story here? If they don't really like each other, why do they stick together? While snakes don't have complex lifelong social structures or societies as we do, it appears there are times and places when snakes have nonpredatory and noncompetitive relationships with each other. And some species are always like that.

So, some snakes do fine with—and may even prefer—company. Others don't. Hey, there are times when we all feel like that. No wonder you love your legless friend. It's just like your two-legged ones.

FOR LIZARD LOVERS
Some female lizards change their coloration to let male lizards know the female is not interested in sex.

When Snakes Prefer Other Family Members to You

Many snake owners and handlers have noticed that snakes show definite preferences for some people—and go out of their way to avoid others. Valesa Linnean, of Alaska, says her Burmese python always hissed at her ex-boyfriend, but when she picks it up, and then puts it back, it "kinda like sighs, almost saying 'Aw mom, do I have to go back?'" When anyone else tries picking it up, "It gets pretty nasty, and will actually flinch away from them and hiss."

Other snake owners report similar experiences, reflecting that snakes seem to recognize scents of certain people over time, often preferring to go to them. For example, one snake owner reported when she and her husband are sitting on the couch, their snake will crawl across furniture—and him—to get to her. Although she finds it endearing, her husband does not.

Who the snake gravitates toward may be unrelated to who feeds it. Sharon Bolton's Taiwan beauty wraps itself around her husband, but every time she tries to go for it, it rattles its tail and strikes at her. "Gosh darn it," she complains, "I'm the one who feeds it and cleans the cage. He just takes it out and holds it."

How Smart Are Snakes?

There's an expression that goes "It has an IQ lower than a snake's belly in a wagon rut." Everyone knows a snake's belly is low, but how low are their IQs?

Without an enlarged cerebral hemisphere—the part of the brain that controls learning and thought—snakes don't have higher brain functions, and they're never going to become Ivy League.

Still, they *can* learn certain associations; for example, if you always drop food in their enclosures, they will associate your arrival or opening of the "gates" with an impending meal. Unfortunately, snakes don't always distinguish between the message and the messenger, and they'll bite the first thing that comes in—including your hand if you're not careful.

Still, their learning is a bit more sophisticated than just that food is coming. Some captive snakes learn when it's coming, if they're kept to a regularly scheduled feeding time. Thus, they're ready when their handler or owner approaches with their meal.

Furthermore, a snake may have some sense of who's feeding it, and some can also tell that it's not another snake feeding them, meaning they can distinguish human beings from other types of animals. That may not seem like much, but snakes don't need to know that much.

As someone posting to Slither as "Pythoness" pointed out, "Snakes have a deep evolutionary wisdom. They are creatures that are arrow-simple and don't have a lot of unnecessary frills. That's why they're a symbol of wisdom in many religions the world over."

She continues in the snake's defense. "They can't herd like a sheep dog, or chivvy cattle like a cutting horse, but they don't need to. They have everything they need to keep on doing what they've done for millennia. And they're good at it, even if it does sometimes take half an hour to find the head of a prey. Stupidity to me means not using the intelligence one was born with."

So, your snakes probably aren't as dumb as you think, or as smart as you hoped. Even if you think your snake's a genius, it's really just a creature of instinct and habit, unable to think much or do anything like, say, algebra. Indeed, as one person wryly noted: "The animals snakes eat are a lot smarter than they are—provided they are alive."

How Long Can Snakes Remember, or Fangs for the Memories?

Snakes may not cram for exams or do well on SATs, but that doesn't mean they can't learn lessons. Once bitten, twice shy is like the three Rs for snakes; in other words, some do learn from their mistakes.

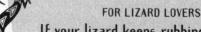

FOR LIZARD LOVERS
If your lizard keeps rubbing its snout against the side of the enclosure as if it's trying to get out, put barriers like plants along the sides of the enclosures.

Some say snakes can remember a lesson for several weeks; some people think snakes' memories last longer than that. For example, the owner of a Burmese python noticed that his snake was hesitant about eating after he swallowed a mouse backward, with disastrous results.

This person wrote to Bill Love, writer, photographer, herpetoculturist, and columnist for *Reptiles*, and said that some snakes become "gun shy" for varying periods of time after being bitten by an aggressive rodent. He said snakes seem to remember such early lessons well, often refusing to fixate on rats for some time after a bad experience.

They say an elephant never forgets, but maybe a snake is a bit of a mental maven in the memory department too.

How to Tame and Train a Snake, or Can You Teach an Old Snake New Tricks?

Charles Mosher explains that:

> There are fewer opportunities to reinforce a snake's behavior than a cat's or dog's, since snakes don't eat every day, and don't have any strong social instincts you can exploit, like a dog has. The only positive reinforcements for snakes are feeding, being at the right temperature, and being touched appropriately.

Here are some training secrets experts suggest:

- Start out slowly, since you don't want to frighten the snake from the beginning.

- Don't push past the snake's point of comfort. If you pay attention to it, you'll soon learn when it is comfortable and when it is not.

- Once the snake tolerates you walking by its cage, changing the water bowl, feeding, and cleaning, you can try touching it gently.

- Then, hold the snake for a few minutes at a time, a few times a day.

- When (and if) the snake has gotten to the point that it doesn't try to slither away after you pick it up, try taking it out of the cage and actually holding it outside. It will probably squirm or try to get away, so hold it gently until it calms down and realizes that you're not going to eat it.

Stinky Snake Tricks

Snakes can't learn tricks, like jumping through hoops, or, more appropriately, slipping under them. But snakes can learn to behave in a particular manner if certain things are done to them.

For example, some snakes, when upset or when someone holds them, "musk," emitting a foul self-defensive odor from musk glands at the base of their tails. (Don't wonder; you'll know when it happens.)

If you quickly put the snake back into its cage every time it sprays, an antisocial snake will learn this "trick" of musking people to get them to leave it alone, says Lenny Flank in *The Snake: An Owner's Guide to a Happy Healthy Pet.*

Now, that really stinks. So learn to put up with it, or your snake may make you the butt of its jokes.

Do Snakes Like Cats and Dogs?

Occasional news reports of snakes eating dogs aside—as if dog lovers could forget—few snake owners with dogs have reported serious problems, but many with cats have had difficulties. In some cases the snake seems to go after the cat; in others the cat goes after the snake.

FOR LIZARD LOVERS
Pick up a lizard by cupping your hand under its belly, with its rear end resting on your wrist or arm.

As Wayne Chandler says: "The best bet seems to be to not let the two out together, not just for the sake of the cat, but because cats are in some ways just as predatory as snakes."

Still, he reports—and others have echoed this—that while his cat and snake were initially curious about each other, they now get along fine, although he doesn't let them out together. "When we first got the snake, Edward (the cat) spent a couple of nights sitting in front of the cage watching, but now he and the snake pretty much ignore each other.

"The only real difficulty I've had is convincing Edward that the mice I bring home are not for him," he added.

Says Valessa Linnean: "I believe that we teach our snakes what is food—my Burmese was rather confused when I first gave him a quail, but now the smell of birds makes him come slithering as fast as the smell of rats.

"As long as you are not feeding any of your snakes kittens, there should be no problem. Just make sure to never let them come too close to each other. Always supervise snakes around other pets."

FOR LIZARD LOVERS
Branches may be bleached in a bathtub. Use one cup of bleach per one gallon of water, and then rinse the branches thoroughly with water. To dry the branches, bake them in the oven on low (200°) for an hour or put them out in the sun for a few days.

What Snakes Are Really Telling You— and Vice Versa

What a Snake Is Trying to Say

Ever wonder if your snakes are talking about you? Zigi Blum jokingly admits that "when my six slitherers are hungry, they all turn suddenly when I enter their room, giving me the impression that they've just hastily quit whispering—"shh . . . here she comes!"—in their sinister plans to escape, not to mention eat all the mice they want."

No, your snakes are not talking about you, but they are talking *to* you. Not with sign language of course—no hands—or smoke signals, since neither of you should be playing with fire. But snakes have their own signals, and once you understand them, you and your snake can communicate with each other, making you a better owner and your snake a better pet. (Not to mention drawing the most incredulous stares from family, friends, and strangers alike.)

Here's what they're saying when they do certain things:

- Hiccuping. *OK, it happens to me occasionally and it isn't a big deal. Don't do something dumb like trying to scare me into stopping or putting a bag over my head.*

- Tongue darting back and forth. *Hey, I've found something interesting. Check it out!*

- Closemouthed striking, followed by flattening of the body. Most likely: *Go away.*

- Openmouthed breathing. *Oh boy, am I sick. It's probably my respiratory system. Don't just stand there. Do something about it.*

- Constantly holding head sideways and looking up at the sky. *I told you I was really sick.* When a snake gets into this position, it's called *stargazing* and it's a serious neurological symptom associated with an incurable disease (IBD).

- Constantly soaking in its water bowl. *It's too darned hot in this place.* Or *maybe this will help me drown my miserable little mites.* Or *where did you put my hide box?*

- Lifting itself up like a cobra (when it isn't) and looking around, almost like a dog begging on its hind legs. *Hey, this place is interesting. Wonder if there's any food over there?*

- Click. *I may have respiratory problems, but then again I may not. You got a problem with that?*

- Basking in the sun. *I'm not trying to get a tan; just raise my body temperature.*

- Repeatedly striking at a mouse and then quickly withdrawing. *I'm not really hungry, but I sure love to play.*

- Musking. *I'm not happy, and when I'm not happy, I'll see to it that you're not happy.* (See, snakes aren't that different from people after all.)

Does Your Snake Move Furniture Around Its Home?

Interior decoration, snake style: if you see a snake doing this, it's probably saying: *I like this other place better.* But why?

Charles Mosher says that if a snake "walks" a hide box to another spot on the floor, that spot is the temperature they prefer. "Pay attention to them; they are communicating to you. It's all part of the fun," he says.

"It's amazing how some people will pay no attention to their snake," he continued. "They will ask a human, 'Should I do this?' when they should pay attention to their snake. Try to understand it, and act according to what it tells you.

"I think it helps if you are smarter than the snake," he added wryly.

Why Snakes Rub Their Noses on Cages— and What to Do about It

If you see this happening, don't give your snake a tissue, because it doesn't have allergies. Nose rubbing can mean a lot of things, especially that a snake is preparing to shed. The other meanings—usually connected to a snake's looking for a way out—depend on the circumstances, and on the snake.

Since nose rubbing usually means *something*, you should pay attention to it. Especially if a snake does it so frequently that the scales at the tip of its nose look like they've been worn away or torn off.

If it's *not* preparing to shed, ask yourself these questions:

Is its cage too big, too small, too hot, too cold, too humid, or not humid enough?

Is it healthy? Does it have mites? Is it looking for food and has it been eating well? Is it acting strangely in other ways? Does it have enough hiding places? Perhaps it needs a tree branch to climb on.

On the other hand, is it just looking for a way out? Maybe it doesn't like the way the place smells (its cage, not yours). You may want to change its bedding or substrate, after thoroughly cleaning the cage to change its scent.

Finally, it may be rubbing because snakes have problems grasping the concepts of "transparent and hard." They don't understand the idea of "glass," since they don't encounter it in the wild. So you may want to make the sides of its enclosure opaque by putting cardboard, foil, or Styrofoam around the bottom.

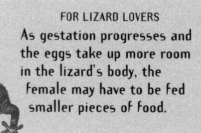

FOR LIZARD LOVERS
As gestation progresses and the eggs take up more room in the lizard's body, the female may have to be fed smaller pieces of food.

Does Your Snake Yawn?
Was It Something You Said?

It's natural for snakes to yawn after they've swallowed food; it helps put their jaw bones back into shape. On the other hand, owners have reported that they've seen their snakes yawn when they're sleepy, when they wake up (just before they start moving after a nap), or when they're hungry, being handled (the open mouth can make their owners slightly nervous), facing a heating source, or just plain bored. Again, snakes are just like people, except they don't have arms, legs, or hair, or wear clothes, jewelry, glasses, etc.

Ho, hum.

The Politically Correct Way to Talk about Snakes

Are you politically correct when you talk about a snake? Do you admit your snake is fat and lazy, or do you say it's horizontally challenged and motivationally deficient?

Since it's important not to offend any group these days, a few snake owners on the Slither mailing list jokingly decided to do some renaming so as not to offend snakes or their owners.

For example, since they were concerned that the term itself, snakes, might be confused with lawyers, one person suggested that a reptilian snake might better be called a "scale-enhanced, length-gifted, appendage-challenged creature."

Since "owning" a pet has a negative proprietary air, it has been suggested that owners could be called "domicile attendants."

To feed a snake would be, "nutritionally empowering" it.

A dead snake would be "life disempowered" or "terminally inconvenienced."

A stupid snake is "intelligence disabled."

And if it's the snake's owner who's stupid or careless, why he or she is just "foresight impaired."

Finally, forgetting to feed a snake would be an "intelligence disabled nutritional incident."

Thus, a sentence like "The snake's stupid owner neglected to take reasonable precautions while feeding his snake, leading to a feeding accident that left the snake dead," would then become "The cold-blooded, legless, scaled life form's intelligence disabled domicile attendant neglected to take reasonable precautions while nutritionally empowering his cold-blooded, legless, scaled life form. This foresight impairedness led to an intelligence disabled nutritional incident, which left the snake life disempowered."

OK, now back to the real world.

Is It Okay to Talk to a Snake?

Most owners who are honest admit that they do indeed talk to their snakes. Some do it for the snake; some for themselves. "I always talk to my snakes in a gentle way when I am picking them up from their enclosures," says an old-time herper. "It makes me more relaxed, so I assume the snakes are then more relaxed. I tell them how pretty they are, and I tell my baby boa how cute and chubby it is." (It's a good thing it's a male he's saying that to; many females would consider being told that they're chubby to be justifiable grounds to bite the speaker.)

In addition to relaxing (or insulting) a snake, talking to them may serve other purposes too. An owner of several snakes admitted he was cheering on one of his male snakes when it was copulating with a female. "Hopefully, it'll take my words of support and get me some viable eggs in a few months."

So, there's nothing to worry about if you talk to your snakes. But if you hear them talk back. . . .

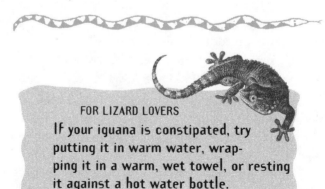

FOR LIZARD LOVERS
If your iguana is constipated, try putting it in warm water, wrapping it in a warm, wet towel, or resting it against a hot water bottle.

Should You Name Your Snake?

Absolutely, say many caring owners. Many people don't, thinking that since their snakes have no ears, and they don't care, there's no point. But as one person posted on the Internet, "I hate talking to other people and having to say 'My albino Cal,' 'my yellow bull.'"

He also wrote that he felt that the lack of names contributed to the image of snakes as poor pets, making people less anxious to view them that way. "When I tell people the names of my animals ('This is Sheldon, my pet rattler'), they become interested in them, especially kids, who then ask questions about the snake." (Like: "Is your snake's name *really* Sheldon?")

Perhaps the best reason for naming snakes was offered by one snake lover from the Midwest who says: "If you have snakes, and have named every one of them, then they are your friends."

Real Snake Slang

Snake books always define boring formal terms for you, like *gravid* and *brumation* and *clutch*. This book isn't boring, and it isn't formal, so here are some *interesting* words and phrases snake people use among themselves that generally aren't defined in books.

Burm: Burmese python

C.B.: Nothing to do with a radio. It means captive-born or captive-bred snake.

Cervical dislocation or bonking: Usually a reference to what's done with mice. You don't want to know any more than that.

Crew: A newborn mouse that has just grown a small patch of fur and looks like it has a crew cut.

Dry bite: A bite that doesn't contain venom.

Fuzzies: Slang for a young mouse just starting to get fur.

Gut loading: Feeding a good meal to the intended food animal before then feeding that animal to the snake.

Hoppers: Adolescent mice, so named because they tend to hop when startled.

Humidity box: A high humidity area for a snake; for example, a plastic box stuffed with semimoist sphagnum moss.

LD_{50}: How venomous the snake is. The lethal dose to kill 50 percent of a population, usually mice.

Mice on ice: Common slang for prekilled frozen mice.

Mouse (or rat) lax: Injecting a prekilled mouse (or rat) with mineral oil, sometimes done to help a constipation problem.

Mousicles: Same as mice on ice.

Pinkys and pinkies: Slang for a newborn mouse that is too young to have fur.

Popped pinkies: Just born mice.

Power feeding: Giving snakes extra food, sometimes by placing more in their mouth just as they're finishing a regular meal.

Pups: Very young rats or mice.

Retic: Reticulated python.

Scenting: Fooling a snake into eating something by mixing it with the scent of something they might prefer.

Screamer: A term used by people selling snakes to indicate that their snakes are outstanding or unusual. "I've got some real screamers here."

SFE: A stupid feeding error, like touching a rabbit before feeding it to your snake.

Spiking: Putting food into something through something else; for example, vitamins may be injected into a dead mouse before being fed to a snake.

W.C.: Wild-caught.

"Hot" Stuff Doesn't Mean Hot Stuff

Reptile Hobbyist ran a letter from a pet-store owner warning people about the meaning of the world *hot*. He said most customers who came into his store didn't know that *hot* meant *venomous*, and they thought it meant popular and desirable. And some people found out the truth too late.

FOR LIZARD LOVERS
Slash (from Guns n' Roses) is a serious lizard lover who has one of the largest private collections in the world—and a full-time animal caretaker to care for them.

A Diamondback Is Not a Girl's Best Friend

Why Some People Recoil from Snakes

Why do most adults have such negative reactions to snakes, while young children often don't? True, the snake got quite a bit of bad press right from the Bible, but the negativity doesn't just derive from exposure to that. After all, more people in America watch TV and movies than read the Bible (or at least they spend more time watching TV than they spend reading the Bible), and it's from the media that most acquire the notion that "snakes are bad."

Generally, the only things people hear about snakes are descriptions of their frightening features. And the only time they hear anything about snakes is when they do something bad—even though it's usually the owner who does something wrong—like when they escape or bite someone. Most people don't even know that snakes perform a valuable function in nature, and may think it's OK to harm or kill snakes.

> **FOR LIZARD LOVERS**
> Some lizards have flattened tails that they use to help them get through water.

Indeed, even the most animal-loving people sometimes think it's all right to kill individual snakes for absolutely no reason whatsoever. The gentle Albert Schweitzer, who trekked around the jungle and wouldn't squash a bug, is reputed to have killed snakes without provocation.

Furthermore, people who would swerve their car so as not to hit a squirrel or a lizard, or any living creature, may go out of their way to run over a snake. Not only that, but they may drive back and forth to make sure the snake is really dead.

Some of this negativity may arise because people think that's the way they're supposed to be. Women, for example, have been led to believe that they're supposed to be afraid of mice, and some act accordingly when they see one. (Eeekkk.)

One way to change the perception of snakes—besides the obvious, emphasizing the good that they do and the benefits of venom—would be to change the image of how people *should* feel about snakes. If people weren't shown to be petrified of all and any snakes, some wouldn't be. If they weren't told that they were supposed to dislike snakes, maybe fewer would feel that way.

Pet Animals That Really Are Dangerous

Want to talk dangerous animals? Most human deaths caused by animals are caused by horses (kicks, falls, etc.), although you almost never hear about that. And the papers rarely report when a dog bites someone, although there may be as many as 750,000 dog bites each year requiring medical attention— approximately ten times the number of rattlesnake bites, yet both kill about the same number of people.

And according to *277 Secrets Your Cat Wants You to Know,* there are 22,000 cases of cat scratch fever people get from their own cats each year, sending the owners to hospitals.

As one frustrated snake owner said, "I have more scars from cat scratches and bites than any other animal, including rodents and birds. Apparently there is no safe pet for idiots. Maybe people should try fish—preferably not piranhas though."

Snakes Aren't Always the Bad Guys

Snakes haven't always been depicted as evil incarnate; even though the best known snake in the Western world is the biblical bad guy in the Garden of Eden, who tempted Eve with an apple, supposedly leading to the downfall of man (and woman).

Snakes have represented knowledge and healing to many groups of people throughout time. Indeed, the reason the medical symbol is a snake wrapped around a cross is that people once thought that snakes could live forever, and that they became rejuvenated each time they underwent brumation (a process similar to hibernation).

Snake Fear Versus Snake Phobia

How pervasive is our fear of snakes? According to one study, snakes frightened more people than any other fear, including public speaking, getting fat—and dying. Some people are so afraid of snakes they can't even eat noodles, because they look like skinny snakes to them.

This fear may be something people learn as they get older, and they can often unlearn it with contact and information. On the other hand, people with *phobias* to snakes may not be able to shed their fears so easily. Phobias are usually more irrational, intractable, and resistant to change, and thus are harder to cure. Dangling a snake in front of a person with a snake phobia is not a good idea. Actually, dangling a snake in front of someone who's just *afraid* of snakes isn't such a great idea either.

FOR LIZARD LOVERS
Leonardo DiCaprio is one of many famous people who have lizards.

Still, people who are phobic are not going to be calmed by seeing a snake, or by your telling them that most snakes aren't harmful, or by your trying to argue logically with them. Nor will they be moved by your thrusting a photo in front of them and saying, "Look how adorable my little retic is."

The best thing is *not* to discuss your hobby with them at all, and to leave helping such people to the professionals. Engage them in discussions of something they're not afraid of, like the weather—or sharks.

Ten Reasons Not to Kill That Backyard Snake

Here's a list herper Daryl Sprout put together, showing people why they should be kinder to snakes:

1. No matter what kind of snake it is, you're too big for it to eat.

2. In many areas, fire ants are already driving snakes out faster than Saint Patrick.

3. Snakes are an excellent deterrent to in-law visits.

4. The average cost of treating an envenomed bite: $15-$20,000.

5. They're one of nature's best ways to reduce commercial and residential pigeon poop.

6. When you live around some of the food chain, you live around all of the food chain.

7. A backyard snake will never offer you an apple.

8. The best use of a snake skin is holding a snake together.

9. Three words: *rodents, rodents, rodents.*

10. Many victims of snakebites were trying to kill the snake at the time.

Why Snakes and Their Owners Get Such Bad Press

Snakes can only handle real bites, not sound bites, and so have not been able to help their own image. And some of their negative press is justified. Some snakes do kill suddenly and cruelly, even if its purpose is defensive.

Although most snakes are shy, a few, like the king cobra, may chase people, and the bushmaster of Central and South Africa, which sometimes grows as long as twelve feet, may attack a human being for no reason.

There's also nothing nice about a snake spitting in someone's eyes, or chasing down its prey after it's already incapacitated it with its venom, or taking victims and throwing them against a wall or rock, as does the indigo snake.

Some snake names also don't help their image, although that isn't the snake's fault, since they didn't bestow it on themselves. Still, how positively can one view any animal called a death adder, saw-scaled viper, or fierce snake?

There are other ways, too, that our language adds to and reflects the negative image of snakes. We talk about "snakes in the grass" and it's not a compliment. Lawyers, an often-hated two-legged species of animal, are sometimes called snakes, as

FOR LIZARD LOVERS
The stress factors that affect chameleons (for example, glass cages, too many chameleons kept together, and being handled) may only affect captured chameleons and their captive-bred offspring. Third-generation captive chameleons don't seem to be bothered by these factors.

are other disliked beings. People who are lying are said to speak with a "forked tongue." Malicious comments are said to be "venomous."

Perhaps the reason some people are so negative toward snakes was best expressed by Jack Horner, paleontologist at the Museum of the Rockies. "I think reptiles have an undeserved bad reputation because they're different than we are," he said on a Discovery documentary.

FOR LIZARD LOVERS
Even if you blindfold a chameleon, it will still change colors to match its environment.

"We look at a cat or a dog. They get our slippers or newspaper, and we can tell when it's sad or mad. Mammals you can tell something about its emotions. You can't do that with a reptile."

Not All Good Snakes Are Dead Snakes

In the United States, generally the only time snakes make the news is when they've escaped, bitten someone, or been illegally smuggled into the country. But people in some countries view snakes more positively.

In New South Wales, it was still big news when a woman's nine-week-old puppy became lunch for a carpet python. But the follow-up to this news story was quite different from what generally happens there.

The media reported later that most of the calls to the station were not about the puppy, but how the snake was.

Furthermore, the person who related this story later learned privately that callers to the station were told that while the woman killed the snake, they didn't want to include that in their news report, because they didn't want to encourage people to slaughter snakes.

The Image of Snake Owners

The image of those who own snakes is sometimes as negative as that of snakes themselves. Even though snake owners come from all parts of society and comprise all kinds of people, some people think there must be something the matter with those who own snakes.

Ray Miller's neighbor found an almost-dead pigeon on her lawn, and called Ray and asked him to come over and kill it— presumably thinking that because he owned a snake, he wouldn't mind killing an animal.

Why Snakes Are Better Than Dogs and Cats As Pets

Even if you're a fuzzy mammal person, you've got to admit that snakes have certain advantages—especially on a cold winter night when you've got to get up because of your dog or cat. Here are a few advantages of having a snake as a pet:

- You don't have to walk a snake three times a day.
- You don't have to clean a litter box each day.
- If you forget to feed your snake one day, it probably won't matter.
- They shed all in one piece, so they don't cause allergy problems.
- They're generally inexpensive.
- They don't bark or meow, or generally make any noise at all.
- They're happy in small confined areas.
- You don't have to buy them a lot of expensive toys.
- They don't get rabies.

FOR LIZARD LOVERS
Some lizards can be wormed by putting the product on what they eat, so they really worm themselves.

• You can go away for a while and your snake doesn't care.

• They don't scratch your furniture or ruin your carpet.

• They don't die on you frequently like fish.

Even so, snakes don't necessarily make the world's greatest pets for everyone. As Bill Haast of the Miami Serpentarium once said: "You could have a snake for thirty years and the second you leave his cage door cracked it's gone. And it won't come back to you unless you're holding a mouse in your teeth."

FOR LIZARD LOVERS
Geckos have been used in Indonesia to steal hats. The lizards are lowered from windows, and they grab the hat off the victim.

Problems with Neighbors, Spouses, and Others

How to Convince Your Mate to Let You Get Just One More Snake

"Have your mates told you that they will shave their heads, change their names, and flee the country if they see one more herp enclosure squeeze its way into your home?" asked Leigh Kleiman of the West New York Herpetological Society.

If you feel like you can never have enough of the scaly babies, here's a few things she suggests that you can say to your spouse that might work:

- Tell them you want to have a baby. Once the shock dies down, say, "Well I guess I could settle for a corn snake."

- Get rid of the bed in the guest bedroom. "Chances are, no one is willing to sleep there anyway, and it leaves room for many enclosure possibilities."

- Start breeding your own rodents. Have a few conveniently escape and tell your mate: "Gee, population control would be a snap if we only had a few more snakes."

- Tell your mate that you're becoming a vegetarian. Then point out how much more room there will be in the freezer for snake food after the steaks and chicken breasts are gone.

- Point out how empty the top of that low bookshelf looks, and how, from a decorator's view, another viv would sure spice it up.

- Beg. "Shameless, I know, but trust me. I've tried everything on this list and that's the only one that has ever worked."

Although people generally think it's the man who has to plead with his spouse to get more snakes, as in the above instance, there are many cases of women who'd like their husbands to agree to more snakes. As one says of her significant other: "He is the one who holds me back and says 'nonono' when I'm drooling over cute lil baby retics and burms."

Is there anything you can do to get your significant other to like snakes if he or she doesn't? Some espouse spouse "desensitization." To do this:

- Find your local herp club and take him or her and the kids to it.

- Have a few sympathetic larger snake owners talk to them.

- Buy a baby or younger starter snake once they say yes to snakes.

- Encourage the family to handle the snake a lot.

More and More Women Are Becoming Snake Owners

Leigh Carducci echoes what many people are noticing: "There are more women involved in herps than ever before. When I was president of the Western New York Herpetological Society, all of our executive board members were women.

"I had a friend who joined the group hoping to meet a herp-friendly mate. She was disappointed to find the girls out-numbered the boys by at least two to one.

"And, at a recent reptile show, even the breeders were commenting that they'd never seen so many women handling and buying snakes before. I also noticed a surprising number of enthusiastic women dragging their unwilling menfolk around the vendor tables," she said.

Who's Who of Snakes

People with great garters, cute cobras, or ravishing rattlers were once able to enter their pets in *Who's Who of Animals*. This vanity encyclopedia, in addition to the usual dogs and cats, also contained the biography of a python, and some other illustrious snakes.

Unfortunately, the book is now out of print, and no future editions are planned. So your beloved pet snake will just have to continue to live its life in relative obscurity until someone else comes along with a similar publishing gimmick.

How to Tell Your Neighbors That You Have a Snake

Don't just come out and say something like: "Hey I just got the cutest boa constrictor. Want to see it?" Do that, and you may have to pick up the pieces if the person collapses—or pick up the pieces of your furniture if you end up tossed out of your building.

But you *do* have to tell your neighbor somehow. Not just because it's the right thing to do, but because it's best for your snake. Otherwise, one night your snake might disappear from your place and show up in their john when they get up to go in the middle of the night, and they could end up dispatching it—or vice versa.

It's best to build up to the subject slowly, seeing what their reaction to snakes is initially before you spill your secret. For example, you can start by casually talking about snakes you saw on a TV show (no doubt on Discovery or Animal

SNAKE BITES
When a snake is born with two heads, they fight each other for food.

Planet) and gauge their reaction to that. Or, you might mention that you used to keep snakes as a child and see if they're receptive to your reminiscences.

If any of this goes well, you might then say that you're *thinking* of getting a snake—even if you've got a dozen hidden in your home right now. (After all, you probably are thinking of getting another snake.) Your neighbor's reaction might surprise you. As Cynthia Merritt said: "The lady next door doesn't mind my snakes because the cracked-out housebreakers down the street don't mess with the place anymore."

A Snake Owner's Revenge

John D. White, who has maintained and bred reptiles for thirty years, tells the amusing story of a real estate agent who was ready to close a deal on the empty house next to his when her client saw one of his large snakes—and freaked out.

When the agent complained later to John, he graciously gave her his phone number so she could call him in advance the next time she planned to show the house, and he promised to keep his snakes out of view.

Instead of calling John, however, she called the police, the animal control department, the health department, and the

child protective services, lying about John, his snakes, and his family. She told them that "Endangered venomous snakes were living in unsanitary conditions with John White's wife and three children." Not only did John keep his snakes in good surroundings, but he had no wife or kids.

John's revenge later? Whenever he saw this mendacious agent next door showing a potential client the house, he would run outside and loudly shout: "Anyone seen my thirty-foot python?" Or "Where did my rattlesnake disappear to?"

How to Get Your Landlord to Let You Have a Snake

Don't spring your snake on someone—literally or otherwise. When dealing with potential landlords, it may be best not to just come out and use the *S* word at all, if you don't know what the building's policy about pets is.

Start by asking if "cage pets" are OK. If they don't ask what kind, don't tell; if they do ask, after telling them, quickly point out that snakes (unlike dogs and cats) won't damage their property.

FOR LIZARD LOVERS
Some male lizards sneak up on female lizards and try to mate with them while the dominant male is busy.

But if the landlord is still concerned, if permissible, offer a small additional refundable security deposit to keep if your snake does any damage. Your landlord may be able to resist snakes, but what landlord can resist extra money?

Once you and your snakes are legally settled in, be absolutely model tenants, paying the rent on time, possibly even early. And while it may be fine if you occasionally go out for a night on the town, make sure your snake doesn't. One problem with a neighbor could be enough to make both you and your snake homeless, and you'll have to start talking to landlords all over again.

A Few Moral Questions for Herpers to Ponder

Here are some comments that appeared on the Slither list, reflecting areas of concern for sensitive herpers:

Should you breed snakes, which brings the prices down, so that people who don't know what they're doing can have snakes? When everyone's breeding them, doesn't this "Risk driving the prices down to where any knucklehead with $25 can pick up a ball python?"

Should you have a snake if you don't know what you're doing? Novices (or idiots) "may have snakes who go out and terrorize someone's five-pound dog, ending up on the evening news when the snake confuses the dog for supper, making all pet snakes look bad."

Is it necessary to breed snakes at all, unless they're oddball or uncommon?

Should you adopt rather than buy a snake, considering all the unwanted snakes that are out there?

If you're bitten, should you not make a big thing of it, especially to your doctor, so that legislation forbidding your pet becomes more likely?

Should people keep venomous snakes in a residential dwelling, where their escape poses a threat to family and neighbors, and their handling poses a threat to their owner?

Should venomous snakes be banned altogether, so they don't hurt their owners, others, and the image of snakes if they escape?

Should there be no regulation concerning snakes at all?

What about people who sell snakes to others without telling them that they're going to grow quite large and/or dangerous? Is it the dealer's responsibility to tell all? Should there be mandatory information sheets? Waiting periods? Limits to what people can purchase?

"How do you balance the rights of the individual versus the rights of other individuals who don't want to step on a python when they go out for their morning paper?" one asked.

And finally, does every plant or animal that we allow to become extinct bring us a little closer to our own extinction?

Ponty Python

Pope John Paul II is personally petless, but he became a hero to herpers in January of 1998 when he actually blessed a python. He was holding a papal audience that included 100 members of an American circus, and he stopped to pass his hand lightly over a beautiful albino Burmese python's head.

This was reported by AFP, which concluded by saying that "the snake, wrapped round its handler's neck, contented itself by sticking out its tongue." (Which in snake language is not an insult.)

Losing Your Snake—Temporarily and Permanently

How to Find a Lost Snake

Even if you think your security is perfect and that no snake would ever be able to escape, and the conditions at your place are so ideal that no snake would even *want* to leave, think of how much time you put into devising your security system—and how much time a snake has to devise ways to escape.

But you're the smarter one (presumably), so your snake still shouldn't have gotten away. Most snake owners have little tolerance toward those who lose their snake—even if *they're* the ones responsible—since there are ways to ensure that this kind of disaster doesn't happen.

So, you want to catch your snake as fast as possible, which may require more than just looking around. Food will probably help. Bringing a snake out with food is a common method used throughout the world. For example, in Ecuador, they capture lost snakes by tying a dead rodent to a stake. The snake swallows the rodent, including the cord, and is trapped when it becomes attached to the stake.

Forget about the stake, but a good method for finding a snake is to set out food so the odor disseminates throughout the room. Then, put out the kind of supermarket bag that makes a crinkly sound. When the lights are off, and all is quiet, the snake will probably think it's safe to go out and eat. The crinkly sound will give its whereabouts away.

There are other ways, such as wait, and weight. Yes, waiting can be helpful, because you probably won't find your snake right after it disappears, although you must keep looking. But another kind of weight may assist you as well. One owner with a missing snake picked up a stereo speaker, saw nothing, picked up the other, *still* saw nothing—and then realized the second speaker was heavier.

FOR LIZARD LOVERS
Sometimes tails don't break completely, and a lizard is left with a forked tail, which slows it down.

104

Guess where his snake was hiding? Amazingly, their six-footer had crawled into a hole about two inches in diameter, and then curled up around the speaker wires. (And you thought snakes couldn't appreciate fine music!)

Choosing when to look for your snake is also important. Some have found the best time to be at night, a little after the lights are turned off and everything is quiet. Then, to help things along, some people put down a line of flour, dusting the entire floor, following the culprit's tracks in the morning.

You can also use temperature to tempt a snake out; turning the heat on in a cool house to bring them out of hiding. But don't overdo this.

Some also claim night goggles have worked, and since you probably don't have any around, you might want to buy them now so you're prepared if you need them later. (If you don't mind spending a lot of money and looking like a nutty survivalist.)

Finally, the important thing is not to give up looking. One pet snake was missing for five weeks, when the waif sheepishly came out from behind a kitchen cabinet. Perhaps it had gone into burmation, or maybe found another home it thought it liked better—and then changed its mind.

One Way to Get Rid of an Unwanted Houseguest, or a Snake in the Can

This really happened, folks. An old college chum came to visit someone who owned a snake. The owner told his houseguest that he had to be very careful not to let the snake escape, because the snake liked to hide inside the toilet of their one-bathroom home. (Snakes do like dark, warm, and humid places to hide.)

The next day, the snake was gone from its viv. The owner diligently searched all over the house for it but couldn't find it. The houseguest was so nervous about using the toilet that he cut his visit short and went home.

Perhaps this gives you an idea for the next time your mother-in-law visits. . . .

Lost Snakes Are Usually Where They Can't Be

Where do you look for a snake? As one herper, quoted on Bill East's FAQ for rec.pets.herp said: "Assume that your herp can levitate, walk through walls, cloud your mind so that you cannot see it, and gravitate unerringly to the most inaccessible spot in your home."

Indeed, your errant snake will probably be exactly where you think it can't be: in closed desk drawers, tissue boxes, inside nested trays you thought it couldn't possibly get into. A baby corn was found inside nested trays with seemingly no space between them, after the entire stack had been moved several times by the owner looking for the snake.

Under and in back of refrigerators are also favorite hiding spots, but don't try to pull a snake out from there, because of the sharp edges on the condenser fins. Instead, drum your fingers on the snake's tail, which will drive it out.

FOR LIZARD LOVERS
If skin remains at the end of your lizard's toes, soak its foot briefly in warm water. Or, allow the lizard to run on damp bath toweling and them remove the skin.

Some snakes like to poop in the fireplace, where the ashes hide the smell. Thus, fireplaces are another good place to look for snakes—and check your fireplace before you start a fire, if you don't know where your snake is.

Even though the snake may be in a faraway inaccessible place, it's best to start looking nearby. As one knowledgeable owner said: "A lost snake often holes up in a secure, tight cubbyhole in the same room they were in. Their hiding place is usually arrived at by the snake traveling along the baseboard, either left or right from its usual enclosure. I have almost always been successful in finding mine within fifteen feet of their enclosure."

SNAKE BITES
There may be as many as 10,000 illegally owned venomous snakes in private residences in America.

How to Make Sure Your Snake Won't Escape

Make sure the housing is done properly in the first place, with double screening, thick-tempered glass, etc. Also:

- Look for weak spots every single time you clean the cages.
- Take care of those weak spots now. No procrastination.
- Close and lock the cages every time you open them.

Eric Stenström, who offered the above, added: "Not everyone has the skills needed to build safe cages. But everyone who wants a potentially dangerous animal can find someone who will help them do it. They are irresponsible if they don't. Period."

Are Sliding Doors Safe?

While sliding glass doors provide easy access for cleaning a cage, they may also provide a quick escape route for a wily reptile—especially a hatchling, who can go a-slipping and a-sliding right out of its cage.

Natural escape artists, these young ones can be quick to break free, working their way between the panes of sliding doors. They can then easily escape—or become stuck—since sliding doors can have close to a 1/4-inch gap between the front and back glass panels.

Here are some methods people have used to close that gap:

- Running a bead of hot glue down the inside of the outer panel. (Exercise care—sealant with fumes could be dangerous.) Hot glue is fast, safe, toxin-free, smell-free, and leaves no sharp edges. Well worth the cost of a hot glue gun, say those who've bought it.

- Putting both panes in the same groove or track, and securing them with two thin cleats, one on the top, and one on the bottom, so that only one glass can slide.

- Purchasing a long E-shaped piece of metal that fits onto each piece of glass and interlocks so the pieces can't slide.

Should You Tape a Cage?

You're best off saving tape for your parcels. As Jennifer Nelson, an environmental engineer from Anchorage, Alaska, who has seven boas, says: "Avoid masking tape usage at all costs. I have a rosy boa saved from a previous owner who had resorted to trying to keep it in its cage by putting tape around the lid. It still has scars from it."

Masking tape can vary greatly in stickiness. If you must use any—after all, losing a few scales is preferable to death—taping should be a last option. It may take as many as three sheds to get the scars off that can be left after pulling tape off a snake—and once in a while it doesn't come off at all.

If you have to use tape, the best way to remove it is with vegetable oil, margarine, butter, or Pam spray.

Please Don't Flush a Dying Snake Down the Toilet

It's hard to believe that anyone who likes snakes enough to be reading this book would try to get rid of their pet in such a callous and gross manner, but maybe they're considering it because they think a quick flush isn't that bad. They're wrong. A snake can die a slow and vile death from it.

And this isn't the only method that can cause anguish. World-famous veterinarian and vet columnist for *Reptiles*, Dr. Douglas Mader, M.S., D.V.M., D.A.B.V.P. (how's that for credits?), says the following methods for disposing of a snake are also inhumane and to be avoided:

- Cutting off its head. The brain continues living anywhere from a few minutes to an hour, and the snake can feel pain during this time.

- Hitting the snake with anything.

- Putting it in the refrigerator, erroneously believing it's a kinder death than putting it in the freezer. It isn't.

What *should* you do if your snake slips from his mortal coil?

If it's a do-it-yourself euthanasia, the most humane way is to freeze your snake. No, it won't be like falling into an ice river for them. Since they're cold-blooded creatures, they will go into a hibernation-like state from which they will never awaken.

If you have to do this (boo-hoo), Dr. Mader says to put your snake in a clean bag or a pillowcase, and put that in a clean sweater box. Freeze this overnight. And if you live with someone, don't forget to tell them what's in there. Some people think the only thing worse than a live snake is a dead one.

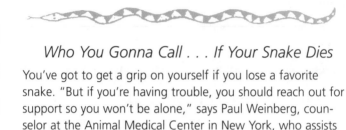

Who You Gonna Call . . . If Your Snake Dies

You've got to get a grip on yourself if you lose a favorite snake. "But if you're having trouble, you should reach out for support so you won't be alone," says Paul Weinberg, counselor at the Animal Medical Center in New York, who assists people who have lost their pets.

Here's a pet support hotline you can call at no charge: (530) 752-4200, 6:30 P.M. until 9:30 P.M. Pacific time, Monday through Friday.

How to Give a Snake Away

If you're moving, overwhelmed, having problems with a snake-hating or snake-fearing partner, or whatever, you may have to find a happy new home for your snake or snakes.

FOR LIZARD LOVERS
During fights among chameleons, the loser may turn a different color.

What to do bothers many people, one of whom wrote *Reptiles* asking for help in finding homes for herps. The reply was penned by the editor, Philip Samuelson, who explained that there was a time when zoos gladly took in exotic snakes, maybe even paying people in the process. Not anymore, so you'll have to find some other place.

You could give your snake to someone as a gift, but make sure the recipient knows about this in advance—and wants it.

You could also try to sell your snake. Many people will pay top dollar for certain species, but make sure the snake is legal in the state it's going to before you do this.

And speaking of legal, there's also another kind of law that matters here. The law of supply and demand. Although rarer varieties are always in demand, especially to breeders, there may be fewer options for what to do with common snakes. Here's what Samuelson suggests:

- Contact your local herpetological society, which may have an adoption program.

- Some animal shelters now take in unwanted snakes, so call those near you.

- Pet stores. If you're lucky, and they have room, they may take them.

Taking Photos of Your Snake Is a Snap

So, you want to photograph your snakes so it'll be harder for one to disappear. Or maybe it's your snake who wants to be in pictures? Or, at least, in a portrait suitable for framing? How do you get a snake to smile and say "mouse"? The best method would be to treat your snake like a temperamental Hollywood star. That is, leave it alone and work around it, especially if you've got an active or dangerous snake.

John D. White, who currently has over 100 reptiles, suggests that, if possible, leave your snake in its tank or transport it to a very clean glass aquarium.

- To reduce reflections caused by the glass, use a haze filter on your camera's lens.

- If you want a classic coiled shot, coax your snake into a bottomless hide box. When it crawls in, lift the box and quickly take your photo.

- You may also want to refrigerate your snake. It sounds cruel, and it is certainly inadvisable for subtropical or tropical species, but some suggest that a cold trip to the ice box for a very short time, will slow down your pet and allow you the time to get the money shot.

The Long and Short of Measuring Snakes

If you want to get an accurate measurement of the length of your midsized snake, don't attempt to measure it from its shed skin, which tends to be between 10 and even 20 to 30 percent longer than the actual snake.

And don't use something stiff for measuring, like a ruler, since you're trying to determine the length of a wiggling coiled-up pet. Two successful methods:

- Running a string down the length of the snake, and then measuring the string. (A monofilament fish line stretches and kinks less.)

- If you can put your snake next to a wall, it will likely crawl along it, stretching out to its full length. Then, stick markers at the head and tail and measure away.

FOR LIZARD LOVERS
If you want a pet lizard that tolerates frequent handling, your best choices are Australian blue-tongued skinks, Australian bearded dragons, and green iguanas raised in captivity.

Taking Your Snake Out of Your House

How to Travel with a Dangerous Snake

Allen Hunter, a herpetoculturist specializing in dangerous snakes, knows of one instance in which people transported a spitting cobra in a Rubbermaid garbage can, held closed with only four pieces of duct tape.

And if that seems incredible, another time, someone put two saw-scaled vipers in a paper bag and left them on a countertop in a bank while he was cashing a check!

Here's what he says people must do when transporting dangerous snakes:

- Never transport "hot" snakes on the public transportation system. It doesn't take a genius to imagine the potential mayhem.

- Always transport snakes by car. Place the box on the floor or on the back seat, strapped in with the seatbelt so the box doesn't slide around and can't be tipped over during a sharp turn.

- Bring along a couple of hooks, just in case.

- Don't dawdle. "Do not pass go, do not collect $200. Go directly home. This means not stopping for beer and leaving your car running outside to keep the snakes warm. A car thief would be in for a nasty surprise later on—and legally, so might you if the thief gets bitten."

> **FOR LIZARD LOVERS**
> Look at a lizard's eyes to see if it is nocturnal or diurnal. Generally, the pupils are vertical or slit-shaped in nocturnal lizards and round in diurnal lizards.

How to Ship a Snake

Please note that it is illegal to send snakes through the U.S. Mail. If you're going to ship a snake, here are some tips for using some other type of carrier, mostly from *Reptile & Amphibian* magazine:

- Don't ship during extreme weather. Tropical species should not be shipped in the winter; heat waves may be dangerous to other snakes.

- Keep snakes at a fairly constant temperature. Styrofoam-lined boxes are a popular choice. During the winter, make sure the shipper adds a few heat packs.

- Have snakes individually wrapped. Although shipping costs can be cut considerably by sending more than one animal at a time, keep them separate. Use coffee cups, shoe boxes, or snake bags inside a larger Styrofoam-lined box. Surround these with bubble wrap, crumpled newspaper, or Styrofoam peanuts. Don't forget the holes for ventilation.

- Mark the outside of your box clearly with something like "Live Animals." It's probably better not to be too specific as to what kind.

  Some people think you should also put "Keep Warm" on the outside of the box, since a brief chill is enough to lead to fatal pneumonia. But since a few minutes in direct sunlight can also lead to death, you never know what some dodos might do if they saw instructions somewhere to keep something warm.

- Put arrows and the word *top* where the top of the box is. No one knows if snakes mind traveling on their heads, but there's no reason to assume they would.

- Know your snake's estimated time of arrival and be there waiting to pick it up. Leaving animals unattended for any period of time increases the risks.

- Thank the mail carrier who delivers your pet. He or she needs the encouragement. Snake handling may be one more reason why an occasional postal worker goes, well, postal.

Dashing Off to Ship a Snake

Certain carriers—such as the U.S. postal service—can't legally transport snakes, so you'll have to go someplace else. Air freight is more expensive, but safer, and there's usually a guaranteed same-day delivery, with one person checking the package in, and another picking it up. Delta is considered the most snake-friendly, especially Delta-Dash, a fast, easy way to ship animals, highly thought of by snake owners.

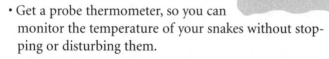

How to Travel with Any Snake

Denise Loving, recording secretary of the Bay Area Amphibian and Reptile Society and a resident of Livermore, California, who has ten pet snakes and breeds Kenyan sand boas, offers the following tips on traveling with snakes:

- Put the snakes in bags inside a Styrofoam ice chest, padded with towels to avoid too must jostling.

- Leave the lid off—except when you stop. Keep the temperature range in the car in the upper 70s to lower 80s Fahrenheit. This is OK for almost any snake, and comfortable for a lightly clad person who isn't moving about.

FOR LIZARD LOVERS
Lizards can often see with their eyes closed.

- Get a probe thermometer, so you can monitor the temperature of your snakes without stopping or disturbing them.

- Try to park in the shade.

- If you're going to be stopped for a long time, put the thermometer where you can read it from outside the car and check it occasionally.

Others who have traveled with their babies offer the following additional ideas:

- If you're traveling in cold weather, use heat packs or hand warmers taped to the inside lid of the box, so they don't come in contact with the snakes and burn them.

- Withhold food for a week before the trip, and for a few days afterward.

- Be prepared. Carry a large tarp to create shade if your car breaks down. The sun beating down on your car could quickly cook your snakes.

Buying a Snake Safely

Purchasing snakes through the mail? Sometimes, suspicious parcels don't tick, they slither. So be sure who you're buying from. Here are a few ways to avoid purchasing problems:

- Reputable stores, breeders, and wholesalers will offer guarantees. Get one.

- Be sure to have any agreement or guarantee in writing before money changes hands.

- Get references.

- If you're going to buy from someone you don't know, especially on the Internet, research them.

Should People Take Their Snakes Out in Public? or Have Snake, Will Travel

How many times have you done a double-take when passing some pedestrian with a pretty boa wrapped around his or her neck—wait, that's no boa, that's a boa constrictor!

OK, not that many snake owners walk around like that. But many would like to, since they're understandably proud of their pets. But do their snakes share their exhibitionist fervor?

Snakes are not show-off creatures in that they'll take a stroll down the avenue—sporting their newest snakeskin bag. They're more likely to keep to themselves. And many people out there strongly believe that that's exactly what they should do. Some lawmakers agree that the best snake is an invisible one, and they've gotten laws passed in certain states specifically prohibiting promenading around with certain pets, like snakes.

Some people are so phobic (ophidophobes) as to suffer panic attacks at the mere *mention* of a snake, let alone a close encounter. Snake owners are wise to be considerate of these unfortunate souls. After all, if your snake frightens someone, it could lead to more fear of snakes, and even less acceptance of people privately owning them.

Also, no matter how well tamed or trained you think your pet is, there have been accidents. Like the time an eight-foot burm latched onto a nine-year-old girl at a festival. Such rare occurrences not only hurt the victim, but the reputation of all snakes and their owners, once the story hits the news.

You also have to consider your snake. Is it really good for you to take it out for a stroll? You are removing the snake from a fixed temperature, possibly placing it around your neck (hopefully a healthy ninety-eight degrees), and most likely subjecting it to drastic changes in temperatures.

For example, you may be going from an air-conditioned room to the midday sun, possibly filled with mad dogs and Englishmen. All this can be quite a shock, not only for those whom you encounter, but for the snake itself, which can cause it to become sick.

FOR LIZARD LOVERS

When some lizards' tails are pulled off by predators, the tail will wiggle for a few minutes to distract the predator, allowing the lizard time to get away. But some lizards' tails, like chameleons', can't be regenerated if broken.

How to Protect Yourself—and Others— If You Take Your Snake Out of Your Home

Alaskan attorney Taryn L. Hook-Merdes, a reptile law expert, says that if you display your snakes in public, and you don't want to get involved in a lawsuit, you should take extra precautions. (Although even then, you may still get clobbered.) Here are some basic things she says you must do:

- Never allow more than two people to touch your pet at once.
- Never leave your snake unattended—don't even turn your back.
- If you display your snake in a cage, lock it securely.
- Place a prominent "DO NOT TOUCH" sign on the cage.
- Be sensitive to people's fears and prejudices about snakes. "Your faithful snake may be someone else's worst nightmare."
- Don't force people to touch your pet, or surprise people with your snakes. "You could find yourself on the receiving end of an emotional distress lawsuit," she warns.

FOR LIZARD LOVERS

Most lizard owners need two lighting systems: one fluorescent, one incandescent. Fluorescent light helps lizards produce vitamin D_3 in their skin, while the incandescent light is used for basking.

Protecting Your Snake, Protecting Yourself

Ten Mistakes Owners Often Make

- Trying to feed your snake unconventional foods. Sarah Beales, who runs Proteus Reptile Rescue in Birmingham, England, was quoted in the *Times of London* as saying: "Often we get vegetarians who fancy reptiles as pets and then say: 'We don't want to feed our snake dead chicks and mice. Can we give it an apple?' I don't think so."

- Just pouring "digestive" type cleaners on rugs to get rid of smells. For these to be fully effective, the treated areas have to be kept wet for almost half a day, and at a certain temperature, and you'll probably still end up with a stain afterwards. Since it's hard to do this exactly right, the smell will probably remain there also.

- Trying to keep a snake, say a python, small by feeding it less or keeping it in a too-small cage. A grown-up starving python can be a very nasty animal. Indeed!

- Putting lightweight bowls in the snake's cage. Instead, use ceramic crocks, which generally can't be tipped, even by larger snakes.

- Leaving an open water container around for your snake. It's usually better to partially cover it, say cut a hole in the lid, which reduces spills and limits humidity buildup.

- Using garbage cans or plastic tubs for big snakes. The handles often aren't sturdy enough if you pick the can up to move it.

- If you're using pillowcases as snake bags, remember that some snakes can burst the bag's seams.

- Snakes can't breathe through some coated bags. Uncoated polyester gym bags are recommended for use as snake bags.

- Not giving a sick snake its antibiotics for long enough, or stopping the medication early if the symptoms disappear. Unless you run the full course of treatment, the bacteria aren't completely destroyed. (The same is true for people taking antibiotics.)

- Putting snakes by the window. Although snakes may like it there, glass increases the sun rays and can make it too hot for them.

When Sunny Gets Blue: Should You Use Sun Block?

The owner of a boa constrictor took his snake to an outdoor show, after which it had two abnormal sheds: the first "rather ratty" and the second one early, also producing a tattered shed almost like a human sunburn peel. His snake also evidenced considerable discomfort immediately after the show for several days, refusing to eat.

Later, he took two boas to an outdoor show, but only handled one, which again showed a similar behavior. Why? On those two shows, he had worn a sunblock (PABA, waterproof SPF #29) and then handled the snake, which later had problems. The person handling the other snake, which showed normal shedding behavior, had not used any block on herself.

Could the snake have been irritated by some ingredient in the sunblock? Until some research is done in this area, you might want to be cautious about applying such products and then handling your snake.

SNAKE BITES
The poisonous copperhead snake smells like fresh cut cucumbers.

Could Your Snake Start a Fire?

This has nothing to do with rubbing two snakes together. It has to do with the possibility that your snake might start a fire in your home. The *Washington Post* reported the story of a suspicious conflagration in a private home in Maryland.

Upon investigation, the arsonist turned out to be an iguana.

It seems the lizard was left home alone in a closet with a heat lamp to keep it warm. The lizard knocked over the lamp, and although it survived unscathed (unscaled?), the conflagration cost $7,000 in damage.

Surprisingly, a fire department spokesman said that this was the *third* iguana-related fire over the past three years.

You can view this as a story suggesting that it's time for iguanas and related animals to get out of the closet. Or you can ask yourself how safe and secure the lighting and wiring is in your house. For example, if your snake got out, could it knock over a halogen lamp, which could cause a major fire?

One final note: Not only could your snake start a fire but you could start a fire because of a snake. A decade ago, a story appeared in *USA Today* about a man from Omaha who saw a snake creep into a hole under his house. This genius rolled up a newspaper, put a match to it, and jammed it into the snake's burrow to kill the snake.

His stupidity was rewarded with a fire that spread throughout his house, causing over $5,000 worth of damage. As it turned out, no one was hurt—including the snake.

This Could Save Your Snake's Life

If your snake has been poisoned, get in touch immediately with your vet, or with the National Animal Poison Control Center in Illinois. It's helpful to know the size and weight of your snake in advance so you can give the vets in charge this information immediately if they need it. They probably will.

There are two ways to get emergency information from them:

- You can call 1-800-548-2423, and they will bill $30 to your credit card.

- You can call 1-900-680-0000, and you'll pay $20 for the first five minutes and $2.95 for each additional minute.

Turning a Wild Snake into a Captive One

Forget for a moment the moral argument about whether or not you should buy a wild snake to begin with or capture one in the wild and try to turn it into your little pet.

There's also the *practical* problem that many such wild snakes never adjust to you or captivity, and don't survive the ordeal because of stress. Stress is not some New-Age psycho-dribble catch-all disease of the month.

Stress can produce a weakening of the snake's immune system, leaving it vulnerable to problems and diseases that may not have seriously affected it in the wild.

Many people don't take the problem seriously or believe that it exists. Why would your little darling be stressed when you've created a wonderful place for it to live in, giving it all the food it wants or needs, not to mention a charming companion like you to go with it?

Your snake may not agree with you. Once, it was a predator, happily eating foods found in the wild. Now, it's often fed an unnatural diet, usually frozen mice. In addition, although you may have placed it in a state-of-the-art abode, that can never, no matter how far advanced, duplicate the free-living environment the snake once had. It is now confused, under artificial lighting, surrounded by unreal objects. ("Is that a *plastic* tree over there? Who do they think they're kidding?")

Furthermore, a snake in the wild wouldn't have interacted with anyone like you. The only time it would have been "handled" was when it was about to become some other animal's dinner. That type of intense life-or-death stress rarely completely goes away.

No matter how mellow a creature you think you are, deep down, your snake may be terrified of you. How would you like it if an alien creature many times your size put you in a cage, fed you a strange diet, and started han-

FOR LIZARD LOVERS
To tame a lizard, build trust by hand-feeding it. Once it allows that, try to pick it up to feed it.

dling you? To the snake you're probably like the Jolly Green Giant, only you're not jolly and you're not green. (Or at least you shouldn't be.)

Protecting Your Pet from Earthquakes—or Listen Up, California Snakes

Melissa Kaplan, snake writer, Internet archivist, and a certified reptile specialist with a master's degree, is concerned about snakes in areas at risk for earthquakes and their aftershocks. So she posted some advice on the Internet about what snake owners can do now before the big one (or even some medium ones) hits.

She first pointed out that such an earthquake could result in "homes collapsing, floors buried under several feet of debris, contents of cabinets and tossed furnishings crushing animal enclosures." And unless you take some precautions like the following, your poor snakes could be at the bottom, or out of luck altogether.

- Prevent enclosures from toppling. Screw hooks into the studs in the wall behind the enclosures.

- Stock up on portable carriers, especially nested ones.

- Keep flashlights, extra batteries, and fire extinguishers in accessible locations around your house—including every room in which you have herps.

- Keep a set of these emergency supplies under your bed "so you don't have to go stumbling around a confusing and debris-filled dark bedroom if something happens during the night."

- Set aside enough drinking water to last a week.

- Have a first-aid kit readily available.

- Pre-designate people to check on your snakes in case disaster strikes when you are not at home.

If you think you don't have room for any of this, Melissa describes a neighbor who has all the extra items "in a large plastic garbage can, sitting in the corner of the bedroom, topped by a circular piece of wood, and covered to the floor with fabric that coordinates with the bedding and curtains, doing double-duty as an occasional table with a lamp next to a chair."

How to Tell One Snake from Another

Some snakes can be very valuable, and to protect their "investments," people tattoo them, clip their scales, microchip them, or photograph them so there's a record of distinctive scale patterns.

Distinctive scale patterns—usually on the belly or the head—are often difficult to discern. People sometimes have to wait until the snake has shed its whole skin—or has died—because of the difficulty of carefully examin-

FOR LIZARD LOVERS
Some lizards have fringes on their toes to give them more traction in loose sand or to help them get across flooded areas.

ing the scales of a live, moving snake—or those of a nonmoving snake who doesn't want to be moved.

Microchipping, or implanting microchips as small as a grain of rice, is an increasingly popular method for identification. Unfortunately, the companies that make this equipment frequently only sell it to licensed vets, so owners and breeders can't do this on their own.

If your vet is going to do it, especially if his or her experience with microchipping animals is limited to dogs and cats, make sure your vet knows to inject the needle slowly between the scales. Although with cats and dogs, faster is better, not so with snakes. They generally contract their muscles trying to escape from the needle, so the needle may have to be kept in for a while before the microchip settles.

How to Tell Boas from Pythons: The Inside Story

Boas and pythons, the oldest species of snakes, are related, and while they're alive, they are almost impossible to tell apart from appearance alone, says Bill Love. Although they do have some differences internally—which can be established after they die—while they're living, the only sure visual test is that pythons generally have slightly different scales under their tails. Most people find it pretty hard to check that and have to wait until after the snake dies to get the real inside story.

How to Hold a Snake—and Five Things to Avoid When Handling One

Melissa Kaplan, who has a website containing dozes of interesting articles on snakes, has a section on how people should hold a snake and give it to others, if you're so inclined:

- Pick it up gently, supporting its body weight in your hands and arms.

- If two or more snakes are intertwined, gently unwrap them as you go for the one you want.

- If you're holding the snake out for others to touch, keep control of its head so you can gently direct it away from the person if he or she appears nervous.

- If you drape the snake around the back of someone's head like a scarf, let them know which side the snake's head is on.

- Watch out for heavy breathing from the snake.

- Watch for heavy breathing from the person—or other signs of nervousness.

What should you avoid when you're handling a snake? Here's what others say about this:

- *How low can you go?* Don't approach a snake from the top. Most predators attack snakes from above it, so if a snake suddenly sees a looming shape swooping down at it, it may act defensively.

- *Heads or tails:* Don't lift a snake by its head, which may cause it to thrash around and be injured. Snakes only have a single ball and socket connection between their skull and spine, and it's easy for this to become separated—which can cause instant death.

- *I'm not ready for my head shot, Mr. DeMille.* Be very careful about touching snakes on the face or head, even if they're tame, says Lenny Flank, who is the author of five books on reptiles, amphibians, and invertebrates, and the source for the above two ideas.

SNAKE BITES
The first casualty of the Civil War was not from a gunshot but a snakebite.

- *(Don't) wake up, you sleepy head!* Don't awaken a snake to handle it or feed it. Some snakes like to wake up slowly and not be startled into reality. How friendly would you be if someone woke you up suddenly to play with you?

- *If you smell like food, you may end up as dinner.* Don't touch food with your bare hands before handling your snake.

- *The end.* If you want to uncoil a snake, do so from the tail to the head.

FOR LIZARD LOVERS
Only two species of lizards are venomous, the gila monster and the beaded lizard, and both are found in the southwestern United States and Mexico.

How to Save Money on Snake Ownership

How to Keep Your Snake Warm in an Emergency

If you live in a cold climate and suffer a power outage, there is no reason to sacrifice your precious friends to an indifferent Mother Nature. While you could buy a generator to provide necessary heat in an emergency, these can be expensive—as well as noisy. (There is a small one available at Home Depot, which would run a space heater in a pinch.) Here are some other ways to keep your snakes warm inexpensively:

- Rocks: These are also decorative in a tank, besides making fine natural heat conductors, which release the stored heat slowly.

- Wrap your tank in towels to help keep the heat in.

- Buy the foot and hand warmers sold in hunting supply stores. These can get very warm, so you have to keep watch.

- Here's a solution that doesn't involve crazy jury-rigged devices or too-familiar relations with cold-blooded creatures. Make a very long extension cord, snake it to a neighbor's home who has a generator, and squeeze their juice. But make sure they give you their permission, or they may release their snakes on you, who might not be as friendly as yours.

SNAKE BITES
Half the people bitten by rattlesnakes never hear a rattle first.

- Keep plastic bottles on hand and, when the need arises, fill them with hot water and put them in with the animals, wrapped in socks or something. This method can also be used when traveling.

• Finally, survivalists will tell you, as will any Boy Scout, to always be prepared. If you live in an earthquake-prone part of the country, you may already have gallon jugs filled with water. In an emergency, warm this water with a gas barbecue grill or fireplace. Then return it to the jug and place in your snake's tank.

Baby, It's Cold Outside

Some prefer a more intimate form of keeping snakes warm: body heat. Many snake owners have battled the cold by bagging their little buddies and placing the snakes quite literally close to their heart. That is, beneath their shirts for a skin-to-scale raising encounter.

If you really get into this, you can cuddle next to a roaring fire, roast marshmallows, and maybe even tell ghost stories, if you don't find that too scary.

Another way to keep a snake warm is to put it in your bed. Again, it's recommended that you bag the snake first, and if you have large unfriendly snakes, don't expect to toss and turn too much.

Does anyone have to tell you that many snakes should *never* be put in your bed? Not only for your snake, but because the snake may refuse your hospitality and visit a neighbor instead. But if you have the kind of pet who'll appreciate sharing your bed and board, and you can do so safely, you may find yourself having the oddest dreams you've ever had.

Snake Power

Just how much power do you use? One poster to the Slither list claimed than when he lived in Seattle, the DEA raided a herper friend of his because his electrical bill was so high all year that they suspected he was raising marijuana.

Imagine the looks on their faces when they opened the freezer and triumphantly pulled out—foil packages of snake food!

Save Money on Hide Boxes

Snakes need to get away from the hustle and bustle of the modern world, just like you do. A snake cage doesn't need to be a prison. OK, it's closer to a cell than a suite at the Waldorf, but a snake can still have its private sanctuary in which to curl up and zone out.

You don't have to go overboard with leather reading chairs and oak-paneled wall coverings, since snakes are relatively unpretentious creatures. Here are a few ideas that will probably make your snake happy—or at least temporarily invisible:

- An old tissue box makes a fine cardboard interior. If you don't want to advertise for Kleenex, you can always cover the box with an eye-pleasing floral design. Some already come that way.

- A plastic salad bowl.

- For a small snake, a toilet paper or paper towel roll. You want to get fancy? Follow the lead of one snake owner who suggests that at the end of the tube, you make little cuts about 1/2 inch in, every half inch all the way around, and fold these little flaps in. These close the tube off, leaving a small but expandable hole for the snake to enter and exit.

- Cardboard boxes from macaroni and cheese type products.

- Shoe boxes with small holes.

- Red clay flowerpots, upside down. Open the drain hole out to a safe size and cut (slowly since clay pots are easy to break) arch doors in the side. These soak up enough water to make a good humid microclimate.

- Empty twelve-pack cardboard containers from Pepsi, or other sodas, can even hold a six-foot-long boa constrictor. Says someone posting as "Reptile" (how appropriate), "If the snake messes in them, it's no big deal to throw them away, which came in really handy when I had a bout with the evil mites. To clean his cage I just waited till my vicious Burmese went inside his box, and picked it up without worrying about getting nailed."

FOR LIZARD LOVERS
Many lizards can see colors.

Three Inexpensive Humidity and Water Containers, or "Snake Saunas"

Inexpensive humidity boxes can be made out of a

- Tupperware or Rubbermaid container, punched with holes on each end.
- An empty margarine container, with holes cut in it, for small snakes.
- An upside down plastic flowerpot, also with holes.
- A small container, like a film canister two-thirds full of water. As the water in the canister evaporates, it keeps the humidity up. Make sure that the snake doesn't tip it over.

Picture This: Saving Money on Housing Decor

One way to fancy up your snake's home is with a tank background. Sure you can purchase these, but you also can be creative and do your own—maybe get your kids to paint a background as a family project—and probably get a lot more pleasure out of it.

If artistic talent is lacking in your genetic background, try buying a print at the local poster store. A nice impressionist painting (perhaps Monet's lily pond series?) could offer your pet hours of quiet meditation and reflection, as well as making a nice fashion statement.

Or, without spending any money, cut out some photos from attractive magazines you find or have around, like *Arizona Highways*, *National Geographic*, or your favorite travel magazine. Cut some cardboard the size of your viv, trim these photos to fit, and paste them on.

A picture can make a big difference. One boa owner from Greece who put a picture of a lush rainforest in his snake's cage found that not only did it brighten the cage, but it made his boa look totally different.

Whatever route you choose to take, do something that expresses yourself, your snake, and your home because you'll have to live with it.

Your snake couldn't care less.

Saving Money on Housing

Having a "snake room" can help reduce costs. And even if you don't have an entire room to spare, you may be able to save money by having a snake *area,* such as a closet. One Texan, for example, has a walk-in closet, and finds that "the ambient temp gets high enough, and the thermostat shuts off the bulbs. The cages are close enough that I can heat separate cages with the same bulbs."

Owning a Snake May Save You Money

There have been plenty of studies showing that people who own pets—generally dogs or cats—are healthier, happier, or whatever they happen to be testing. Usually these studies, and there are dozens like them, only test dog or cat owners.

For a change, a recent year-long survey, reported by *Reptiles,* included snakes and other reptiles. This study looked at the number of visits to doctors made by elderly people who owned pets, including snakes.

Perhaps because pet owners in general experience less stress, they required 16 percent fewer visits to the doctor than those who didn't have pets. This most likely saved them a lot of money—unless they were using HMOs.

Why would owning snakes reduce stress and the number of visits to a doctor? The researchers pointed out that pets provide social interaction, and having someone around to talk to and be with generally makes people happier.

Snake owners may be in an even better position than those owning dogs and cats, because snake owners don't have the stresses of having to walk their pets and spend a lot of out-of-door time with them in inclement weather. Plus snake owners never have to deal with the stress of noise complaints from their neighbors. Even if they have a rattler, the noise won't be loud enough to rattle those living nearby.

The Wild Ones: This Won't Save You Any Money

Generally, it will cost you less to buy wild-bred snakes than captive-born ones. But buying them is a poor way to try to save money because, in the long run, you're likely to spend *more* with all the problems you'll encounter. There may be feeding problems and breeding problems, and wild-born snakes are likely to come loaded with parasites. Enough said?

How to Make More Money When Breeding

Ernie Wagner, author of the *Reptiles,* "Ask the Breeder" column, says that if you're going to breed snakes, once you're past the higher purchase price for an albino or rarer color, it doesn't cost any more to maintain one of these than it does a natural-colored snake.

Although they may look more delicate, the albinos and unusual colors are just as hardy as the normal ones, and the financial rewards when you breed them are usually far greater.

Five Simple Ways to Save Money on Snake Supplies

1. Saving Money on Snake Sticks

Sharon Bolton suggests you use a modified coat hanger, the wire ones that cleaners use to return pants. She says that if you use a regular metal hanger, it's just a single piece of wire at the hook end and it's sharp. Better to use the trousers hangers, which have been doubled over, are sturdier, and won't cut.

These already have a cardboard tube on them, which you remove. You'll see that the metal legs have a little bend at the end; twist them around each other once or twice and you have a perfect handle. The hook is at the other end.

2. Saving Money on Substrate

If you use paper, there are two free sources for it that you may not have thought of:

- Go to the computer room at work and pick up some used computer paper. They'll be glad to get rid of it. Use it print side down.

- Go to your local newspaper office and see if they will give you (or sell you cheaply) roll ends or waste pieces of unprinted paper, which they would have just have thrown away anyway.

Tell them why you want it—like you have seventeen snakes at home to house—and they might even end up doing a story on you. Make sure all your neighbors know about your hobby first.

3. Saving Money on Snake Supplies

You can often get discounts if you buy items in bulk, but you may not have enough snakes to make it worthwhile. If you try to buy these reduced products on your own, the price of shipping smaller orders may erase your savings.

So, get together with other herpers in your area and see if you can chip in to buy together. One place to look for such people is at your local herpetological society. If you don't have one, why not be the one to start it? It's a good way to find out who else has snakes in your neighborhood.

4. Saving Money on Water

Snakes like water, but sometimes water doesn't like them. Some snakes get a white coating on them, probably from excess mineral deposits in the water, which may lead to a possible calcium carbonate buildup on the snake.

What can you do? Bottled water is too high in mineral content to use, and besides, who can afford to keep snakes drenched in Perrier? A reverse osmosis filter may solve your water problems, but this expensive process will drain your bank account.

It has been suggested that a more financially feasible way may be to collect rainwater. It contains no calcium carbonate, is very soft, and is slightly acidic—yummy for a parched reptile.

You may want to boil it first to kill off any bacteria. Then allow it to cool and toast to good times.

5. Saving Money with a Simple Homemade Mite Treatment
One of the safest ways to free your snake of unwanted mites—and it may not cost you anything if you already have the box at home—is the rotating sweater box suggested by John. C. Haudenshield, a Virginia biologist.

Start with two sweater boxes or a similar type of inexpensive plastic container.

Rotate your snake to the new, clean container every day or every other day. Since the mites must leave their host to lay eggs, by cleaning the box each day, you eliminate the possibility of new mites.

Adult mites have an estimated lifespan of about fourteen days, so it is best to continue the treatment for at least two weeks.

Leggo My Eggo!

The problem with commercially produced incubators is that they're expensive, ranging in price from $50 to $200. But Joe Norton, former zoological manager of Conservation Station, at Disney's fabulous new Animal Kingdom, says you can make one yourself with a thermostat, a thermometer, the right-sized aquarium fitted with a plastic lid, and incandescent lightbulbs. To control the humidity, put a small box in the aquarium on a raised surface, with one or two inches of water and an aquarium heater in it.

FOR LIZARD LOVERS
The venom of poisonous lizards could save millions of lives because it causes blood pressures to drop. Unfortunately, lizard venom is in very short supply.

Snakes and Food

"Bulimia" in Snakes

OK, maybe it isn't bulimia in the traditional sense, since snakes don't gorge on a big dinner, worry about whether that's going to cause love handles, and sneak off to the bathroom and throw it up, but snakes *do* throw up quite a bit. Fortunately, most of the time, it's not something to worry about. The main reason for it happening is that the snake hasn't had time to digest its food, placing physical or psychological stress on its system. After all, in the wild, if an enemy approaches—or it thinks one is coming—the snake may have to get rid of its food as fast as it can so it can flee quickly.

> **FOR LIZARD LOVERS**
> Some lizards' eyes move independently, allowing them to look in two different directions at once.

"How would you like to eat all of your meals for one day at the same time—that is a full breakfast, lunch, and dinner—and then go off and wrestle someone immediately afterward?" asks Dr. Douglas Mader.

Alas, the main stress a captive snake is likely to experience after eating is *you*. A common reason for regurgitation is that people often handle a snake too soon after it's eaten or drank something.

Solution: Leave your snake alone when it's digesting its food.

The other reason snakes may throw up—other than physical problems such as obstructions—is because the temperature is too cool for it to be able to properly digest its meal. The food remains in its system, gets bad, and is then thrown up.

The solution again is obvious.

Three Tricks to Make Snakes Eat

If a snake won't eat its prekilled prey:

• Put your snake and its food in a pillowcase or cloth bag—tied, with a folded towel on top—overnight.

• Dip the prey into chicken stock or chicken soup; the chicken soup will probably be good for what ails the snake, too.

• Defrost the snake's food on top of its enclosure, so the scent wafts down into its habitat. Make sure to clean the top afterward.

Mousemaker

Those who have tried "Mousemaker" all seem to be enormously enthusiastic about this concentrate, which gives food the scent of mice. One user said that, since he started using this odor manipulating product, his snake now "inhales his food," when "Zooey used to stare glumly at dinner for an hour."

Another said, when he discovered this product, "My cornies would take nearly an hour to eat and now they strike and eat within two minutes."

Mousemaker is manufactured and sold by T-Rex and is available in pet shops. It's very concentrated, so only put a couple of drops on the food. Just a dab will do ya.

SNAKE BITES
Cleopatra probably committed suicide with an Egyptian cobra, not an asp, as is commonly believed.

Tricks to Get Your Hatchlings to Eat

It's not always easy to get a baby snake to eat, especially a wild-bred one. Lizards, rather than mice, may be the normal diet for them, but how to you get a lizard-loving snakelet to transfer its allegiance?

Here are the standard methods:

• Keep the snake and its food in a small container so the snake can get to it easily.

• Keep the food items small; snakes digest them better.

• Separate hatchlings at food time so shy snakes aren't intimidated by more aggressive ones. (Even species that can be housed together should be separated at feeding time.)

• Place the mouse in a small container with a wild-caught lizard for a few minutes, which will transfer the lizard's scent to the mouse.

• Even if you don't have a whole lizard around to sacrifice, it may be enough to just use a tail, or a piece of their shed skin. And, if you don't just happen to have any lizard skin around— lizard-skin pocketbooks, belts, and shoes don't count—ask your local pet shop if they have any freshly shed lizard skin for you. If so, they may be more than happy to get rid of it by giving it to you.

• Some baby snakes are afraid of adult mice. So if you feed them a prekilled mouse, wash the pinky with mild soap and water. Then rinse it repeatedly to get rid of that fearful smell.

• The "wet-pinky" technique: Allow your "problem feeder" to go without water a little past when it would normally drink it. Soak a prekilled pinky in warm water (90°F) for about an hour. Offer the slightly soggy meal to your snake, who may then drink the moisture off the mouse, eating it in the process.

SNAKE BITES
Over twenty million Americans are said to have reptiles now—mostly snakes.

But you have to be careful because you don't want to overly dehydrate your snake by depriving it of water, or then the whole issue of its not eating could turn into a much worse one of its not breathing.

White or Dark Meat?

Some snakes develop a color preference for their food and will refuse food that isn't that color or size. In most instances, if your snake seems to prefer white mice to brown, it's not a matter of "taste" the way people might choose white meat over dark on chicken or turkey.

Bill Love explains that albino (white) animals are generally uncommon in nature, and are therefore usually easily spotted. So your snake may be seeing the white mice more readily than their brown or beige cousins, giving the impression of preference.

But whatever color you give a snake, if you change it, it might not eat the new prey as rapidly. Indeed, if you usually serve white mice, your snake may pause a moment before accepting a brown mouse—in case more familiar food is tossed in—or strolls by.

FOR LIZARD LOVERS
Select branches with interesting shapes, for the most attractive habitat. Scrub oak branches are a good choice, since they have interesting turns.

How's This for Dieting!

Dave Fulton says that "some snakes go on hunger strikes to upset, annoy, and worry their owners out of pure spite." Here's just how ornery they can get:

- If some snakes in captivity don't get the food that they want, they may starve to death rather than eat something else.

- Snakes may refuse food because they don't like the size of the prey.

- Snakes who are hibernating often go six months without food.

- Some males fast during the mating season.

- Even when they're not hibernating, some snakes routinely go a year—sometimes more—without eating.

- Hatchlings often refuse food until their first shed.

- Female snakes don't eat the whole time they're gestating—which can last from one to more than three months—due to the space taken up in their body by the future snakes-to-be.

- Snakes are diurnal or nocturnal, and if you try to feed them during the opposite period, they may not take food.

Water, Water Everywhere

Unlike warm-blooded pets, who require a constant water supply, reptiles don't need to drink water every day. Assuming that they're feeding regularly, and aren't exposed to warmer than normal temperatures, most healthy snakes have no hydration problems if offered very little water. Indeed, some snakes from arid places can survive even two years without access to it.

Snakes sometimes act rather oddly around water. Some snakes like to soak it in after a meal, and some will drink it off themselves. For example, after one woman sprayed her snake's cage, some of the water landed on her snake's back. It turned around and drank the water off its own body, doing this repeatedly, even though it was right next to its full water dish.

Get a Grip on That Food

Some snakes may need to have their food presented to them with tongs, so they can grab it and constrict it as if it were live prey. Here is what some people have found effective to use for dangling instead of their fingers:

- Hemostats: These are the long tongs used to clamp blood vessels during surgery. They come in a variety of lengths, with several types of clamps. Most recommended is the twelve-inch locking artery forceps, which can be used to get a good grip on the product. When the snake strikes, simply twist the handle and release.

  SNAKE BITES
  Many people bitten by their own pet snakes were drunk at the time.

  These are available by mail order from some snake suppliers, medical supply houses; or, if you live near a university medical school, the campus bookstore may have hemostats.

- "Mechanical Fingers," used by auto mechanics, are both inexpensive—about half the price of a hemostat of comparable length—and practical. About eighteen inches long, this handy tool has a flexible shaft and spring-loaded "jaws" for a good grip.

- Outdoor barbecue tongs are inexpensive and will also get the job done. Just make sure that you have a solid grasp on the object in two places. Also, be careful that the snake doesn't grab these tongs instead of the food or it may end up very hungry.

FOR LIZARD LOVERS
If you have more than one lizard, you should have more than one basking platform.

Strange Things Snakes Eat

Parade magazine reported that an eight-foot boa constrictor named Teardrop, owned by a couple in Oregon, ate its heating pad. They quoted its unnamed vet as saying that the pad probably seemed like food to the snake. It was warm and fuzzy and had some hard objects inside that must have felt something like bones.

When Dinner Bites Back

Oh rats! That's what the snake probably thinks when it realizes—too late—that the rat that was supposed to be its dinner has similar ideas the other way around. The snake's prey sometimes does indeed become the predator, and your snake may become the victim of a boisterous rodent it thought was supposed to be its dinner.

This commonly happens when a rat falsely believes the snake is in a state of hibernation, and incapable of becoming aggressive and eating. Then, if the snake and the live rodent are left unattended, without food for the

> **FOR LIZARD LOVERS**
> Many species of lizards won't drink liquid from a dish. To get them to drink—and create humidity at the same time—regularly sprinkle water in their habitat. This may seem like rain or dew to them. If you spray the sides of the tank, when the drops start moving down slowly, the lizard may drink the water off the sides of the glass.

rodent, the latter may decide that a lethargic snake may not do anything to stop it from a fine feast.

It would almost look funny to see the little rat going for broke, except that a rat bite is serious, even potentially fatal, to a snake. Rodents carry several types of infectious bacteria on their teeth, so lethal they laugh at any antibiotic sent in. ("You puny little drugs think you're going to stop *me?*")

Another reason rat bites are potentially serious is that rodents don't snap and swallow. They have a nasty habit of gnawing when they eat, sort of the way people eat corn. Since snake skin isn't a corncob, serious damage can ensue. So, unless your bitten animal is strong and healthy, and the amount of toxin produced is small, it may absorb these poisons.

FOR LIZARD LOVERS
To choose a good lizard, look at its tail. Healthy lizards generally have fatter tails.

Mite-y Awful, or Getting Rid of Mites, Salmonella, and Other Problems

How to Tell If Your Snake Has (Eccchhhh) Mites

Just because you don't see the mites doesn't mean your snake doesn't have them. Mites hide under scales, often camouflaged by your snake's markings. You can sometimes spot these nasty critters as small dark moving specks between your snake's scales, especially on the legs and lip. The easiest way to spot them, though, is around the eyes, where mites appear as tiny black specks that move.

Mites that have been feeding are about the size of a round pinhead. To see young, unbloated ones, you have to look close. Sometimes you don't see them or their eggs at all. You may only see them *after* they're off your snake; for example, as little black specks in water after your snakes have soaked in it.

Hint: If you put a ceramic bowl in their tank, get a white one, since mites are easier to see against white. You can also monitor for mites in the water bowl itself.

Similarly, using white paper for substrate also makes them easier to find. But even if you use a colored substrate, occasionally leave the snakes overnight on white paper. The next day look for pinhead-sized black specks that move, or white specks (which is their excrement) that don't.

> **FOR LIZARD LOVERS**
> When lizards get new tails, they don't always match the color, size, or texture of the lost ones.

The Worst Snakes for Parasites

Veterinarian Roger J. Klingenberg, author of *Understanding Reptile Parasites*, believes the following are the worst carriers of parasites: imported pythons (especially ball and Indonesian), water and garter snakes, indigo snakes, and most imported Asian snakes (including rat snakes, sunbeam snakes, and vine snakes).

Are No-Pest Strips Safe?

No-pest strips are used by many snake owners—but they shouldn't be. There is evidence that they cause snakes to develop a rapid progressive paralysis and birth defects.

The eminent dean of snake veterinarians, and author of the definitive text, *Reptile Medicine and Surgery*, Dr. Douglas Mader, warns against them, saying that just because they're supposedly as "safe" as flea collars for dogs and cats—although many believe those aren't safe for dogs or cats either—they're not OK for your snake. "Do not assume that what is safe for one animal is safe for your reptile," he warns.

If you absolutely feel that you *have* to use them (why?), read the directions carefully and don't leave the strip in for long.

Getting Rid of Mites

You're not seeing things. Those dots in front of your eyes are real—really disgusting, really bad for your snake, and really dangerous to get rid of. Even though you can't easily see mites, they can do plenty of damage. Infestations of these little devils can weaken your snake by taking blood from it, thereby stressing its immune system, making it more likely it'll get sick or unable to recover if it does become ill.

> **FOR LIZARD LOVERS**
> If your lizard has scratched or damaged the plants in its habitat, don't throw the plants away. Let them grow in your house until they get new leaves.

Unfortunately, there is no completely safe method of mite removal. Flea shampoos and other medicinal treatments can contain harmful additives, and can harm your snake now, and possibly in the future, in ways you don't even know of, and don't want to think of.

Olive oil has been suggested as a safe alternative, but it has a negative effect on shedding, causing the skin to flake off unevenly.

One thing you may be able to do is prevent the disgusting little creatures from coming into your home in the first place. They often sneak in after a trip to the pet store to buy mice. The mites lay eggs, which then find a new host on your unsuspecting snake.

So buy frozen rodents. This enables you to avoid this form of leapfrog (leap-snake?) infestation. Although most snakes prefer live mice, after a while, they may come to view the frozen ones as TV dinners. Price keeps many people from buying frozen mice, but frozen rodents can be ordered in bulk, making them less expensive.

Don't forget to tell anyone who shares your refrigerator what's in the freezer. Otherwise, they may freeze you out.

Mites Get in Their Eyes—Uggghhh

Mites in your snake's eye sockets can be difficult to get rid of, since this is a sensitive area. Massage is the best way—if your snake agrees. If it does, move the scales around its eyes in a circular fashion with your fingers, working the mites out. Once free, you can sweep them off the snake with a soft brush.

FOR LIZARD LOVERS

If you're misting your lizard, do it early in the day so it has time to dry completely before evening, when the temperature may drop and cause the lizard to chill.

Does Your Snake Have Salmonella?

First, keep things in perspective. If you get salmonella from your snake, it doesn't mean you'll become deathly ill. You may even have had salmonella already and just chalked off your symptoms to a case of intestinal flu. (Symptoms of salmonella include sharp stomach pains, fever, and diarrhea that usually lasts from two to five days.)

Anyway, you're probably at greater risk of contracting salmonella from handling raw chicken (which can also pass on salmonella) than from handling your snake—if you practice good hygiene.

Ah, good hygiene. How boring, but how necessary, since there may be far more salmonella bacteria around than you realize. As Steve Grenard points out: "Herps poop in their cages and then roam around in it or touch it, getting microscopic particles on their body."

It's even more dangerous if your snake doesn't stay in its cage, because whenever a reptile "free roams" in your house, it could be spreading salmonella in the most unlikely places.

But does your snake have it to begin with? It's a good idea to start out with the assumption that the salmonella bacteria is present in your snakes, because you can't be sure one way or the other. Even a clinically healthy pet can test positive for salmonella in routine health screens, and false negative problems also abound.

Many reptiles can also be *carriers*, but you can't tell, because they don't actively shed the virus at all times. And you can't simply go ahead and treat snakes, just assuming they are infected, because that may result in resistant salmonella strains arising.

SNAKE BITES
One herper milked over 750,000 snakes over a decade—without being bitten once.

Therefore, it's best to be vigilant, practice safe handling, assume your herps carry salmonella, and act accordingly. Salmonella is a hearty bacterium that lives where it lands: on countertops, cage walls, hands, and even clothing you've worn while handling your snake.

It may be strong, but hopefully you are smart.

Ten Ways to Avoid Salmonella

It can't be repeated enough that you must be scrupulous about washing all household surfaces that could possibly be contaminated by your snake. You must be equally diligent about washing your own hands thoroughly after handling snakes. Especially if you're like so many snake owners who wash their pets in the same sink in which they prepare food, or put them in the same bathtub that you or a family member uses.

Here are some ways to avoid salmonella, mostly from Dr. Mader:

- Never clean cages in the kitchen or any place where you prepare or consume food.

- Never eat, drink, or put anything in your mouth when working with your reptiles.

- Always wash your hands with a disinfectant soap after touching your snakes.

- Keep your disinfectants with your other snake-handling tools, so they'll be in easy reach after handling your snake or any objects it has come in contact with.

- Keep cages clean to minimize transmission of all diseases, not just salmonella.

- If you use your bathtub, and you also put your snakes in it (you do live alone, don't you?), carefully clean your tub after you wash your snakes. (Does someone really have to tell you this?)

- Have your veterinarian examine all sick animals.

- Isolate any snakes that test positive.

- If any animal dies suddenly, have your veterinarian perform an autopsy to check for salmonella.

- Check with your doctor if you believe you've been exposed to the salmonella bacterium.

And finally, if you have snakes—or any other pet, such as lizards, iguanas, or frogs, for that matter—and allow them to roam freely about your house, and then permit your children to crawl in the same space without thoroughly disinfecting it, you should be ashamed of yourself.

A Warning about Hand Gels

More and more people are relying on hand sanitizer gels—the kind you carry around with you that don't need water. But when these were tested by KCCI-TV in Des Moines, Iowa, they found no difference in bacteria counts between those who washed with these and those who didn't wash their hands at all. Yikes.

True, some brands were more effective than others. Purell and Alco-Gel, and those containing about 60 percent alcohol, did perform better than the rest. Even with these, though, you have to put a lot of gel on your hands and leave it to dry without wiping it off.

And don't expect immediate results. If you touch your snake, and then put on the gel, wait before eating something with your fingers. Organisms get killed over time. Don't expect these gels to kill on contact—when they kill at all.

Safe Snaking

Infants, young children, those with weakened immune systems (HIV, etc.), or those using antibiotics or immunosuppressive drugs should not handle snakes without checking with their physicians first.

In addition, salmonella can be contracted by pregnant moms-to-be, and this can cause septic abortion, premature birth, or the birth of a seriously ill or even stillborn child.

FOR LIZARD LOVERS
Unlike venomous snakes, which inject venom into their victims, the venomous lizard must hold on to its prey for the venom to reach the victim's bloodstream.

Snake Story: 1-2-3 Testing

When a reptile-owning Canadian physician learned that he'd have to pay $87 for his vet to examine a stool sample from his $50 reptile, as a joke, he slipped his pet's droppings through a human lab for a mere $26—putting his own name on the lab requisition form.

Writing to *Reptiles*, the good doctor admitted he had not thought about the consequences of his frugality. "I was a tad embarrassed when my call partner phoned me on the weekend to tell me that I had a salmonella infection.

"Just when I thought I had lived that one down, I received a letter from a community health service, accompanied by a pamphlet on hand washing, food handling, etc."

The doctor finally fessed up and told the lab whose stool sample had been analyzed, causing chuckles all around.

FOR LIZARD LOVERS

If your lizard needs more heat, put a heating pad for people under the tank and make sure the heat has no way to escape from the top of the enclosure.

Fat, Shedding, or Constipated Snakes, and Other Health Problems

Snakes Who Like Food Too Much

Is your viper too voluptuous? Your ribbon snake Rubenesque? If so, your snake may be too fat from too much rich food and laying around his house watching TV. Oh no wait, that may be you.

Seriously, "pleasingly plump" snakes, like people, also carry a health risk. Like their human counterparts, they're more prone to injuries, pressure sores, skin problems, breeding difficulties, dangerous strain on the cardiovascular system, and even diabetes.

Why does fat happen to snakes? For the same reasons fat happens to people: The snake is eating too much and exercising too little. But you can do something about it. If overfeeding isn't the cause, first have your snake checked out by a veterinarian to make sure there isn't a medical cause, like hypothyroidism or a pituitary gland disease.

If it (probably) is overfeeding, don't start *underfeeding*. Yes, diets do work, but they must be carefully supervised by a professional. Don't try any crash diets. It's fine to feed overfed snakes less, but remember, just like for two-legged folk, rapid weight loss can be lethal. Trying to starve a snake to make it thinner could instead make it sicker.

FOR LIZARD LOVERS
A few species of lizards
protect themselves by making
believe they're dead.

How to Tell If Your Snake Is Too Fat

If your snake is going hog wild over food and you don't have a hog snake, here's how to tell if it's too fat, according to Dr. John Rossi, author of an easy-to-follow book on the physical problems of snakes, *What's Wrong With My Snake?* You can tell that your snake is overweight if it

- has exposed skin between the scales;

- is unable to coil properly;

- has "fat lines," or vertical folds in the scales, created when a heavy snake remains coiled for long periods of time, similar to people's "love handles" or "inner tubes."

Snake Aerobics, or Slithering to the Oldies

Since cottage cheese and liposuction is not an option for your snake, it's time to shape that snake up before it ships out. Fortunately, getting your snake to exercise could be easier than getting you to do the same.

In fact, you could even put your snake on a treadmill. That may seem like a ridiculous notion, but it was actually done by University of California researchers, who put snakes into a tunnel-like treadmill and fitted them with clear little oxygen masks to test their energy expenditure.

But there is an easier way to get your snake to exercise. All you've got to

FOR LIZARD LOVERS
If your lizard's home is outside, watch out for ants, which may be attracted to dead insects, baby food, or other items you're feeding your pet. Ants can swarm and kill baby lizards. Put petroleum jelly on the outer sides of the enclosure, so the ants can't climb up. Also suggested: Put the lizard enclosure on bricks lying in trays of water.

do is make a few changes in its home. Don't expect too much, because snakes can't sustain activity. They wouldn't be able to remain on a treadmill for long, but they could leap on to it quite quickly.

Although exercise is not a substitute for a diet, a good aerobic session will do wonders for your snake's mental as well as physical well-being. Here are some simple ways to get your snake to exercise more:

- For certain snakes, it's enough to add some artificial twigs and climbing places in their viv, so they move around more.

- Let them crawl on you—assuming this is feasible. If you let some constricting snakes crawl on you, you'll be the one who'll end up thinner afterward. So thin no one may ever see you again.

- Put snakes in larger cages, so they have further to travel.

- Space the warm basking area farther apart from the cool, shaded rest area of your tank. (Snakes are ectotherms: They depend on the surrounding temperature to maintain their body temperature. That means they move from hot to cold as it serves their internal thermostat.)

Try the above and, hopefully, you'll end up with a healthy, well-proportioned, yes (gasp) even a svelte, reptile.

Why Snakes Need Exercise

If you were in a cage, cut off from your natural desires and the hunt for food and reproduction, and all your basic needs were taken care of for you, you too would put on quite a paunch. Not many calories are expended by swallowing a farm-raised dead mouse.

In captivity, snakes usually don't move around as much as their free-ranging counterparts. They also eat more frequently, generally consuming larger meals than snakes do in the wild. After all, wild snakes don't have doting humans to dangle food in front of them. Instead, they have to sing—or slink—for their supper.

Tricks to Help a Snake Shed

You should touch a snake after a shed to make sure there are no small bits of retained shed. If so, you may have to do some things to help your snake get rid of it, because leftover skin can harbor disease-causing organisms.

What's a major reason your snake is having shedding problems? You know the old expression: "It's not the heat, it's the humidity." That's true for your snake too, since humidity helps them shed their skins better. Usually the humidity is too low, and the common solution is to raise the moisture level by putting a humidifier in the room or a water bowl at the heated end of the enclosure.

Here are some other methods for removing what's left over, or ensuring a proper shed in the first place:

- Dr. Douglas Mader suggests that larger snakes can be placed in a clean plastic garbage pail, between layers of moist towels. As the snake crawls around, the weight of the damp towels will help remove the loose skin.

- A common method is to put a snake in a damp pillowcase for a while and let it move around in that.

- Or put a snake in a container with tepid water just deep enough to cover its body, but not deep enough so it can drown. Never leave a soaking animal on its own without someone around, or when you return, you may have a sinking feeling that you don't have a snake.

- After a snake has soaked, you can let it twist around you as you hold it in a wet towel.

- Get a Rubbermaid box big enough for the snake to get into. Cut a hole in the top big enough for the snake to get out of. Fill the

FOR LIZARD LOVERS
Nile monitors have been used as "watchlizards" in parts of Africa because they learn to recognize the person who feeds them.

box with damp crumpled newspaper, place the box in your snake's cage, and the snake will go into it, rubbing most of the stuck shed off on its own.

- Place rocks or logs or branches in its habitat, so it can rub against them to help loosen its skin.

- Gently rub its skin with a warm washcloth. Some people use pumice stones to manually remove any stuck shed, but you want to be careful since abrasions caused by the stone could hurt your snake.

Everything should come off cleanly with the above methods, and you must make sure their eyecaps or "spectacles" come off with the shed—without using force—in one pleasing piece, with no sweat.

If They're Not Shedding

- Check that there's water in the snake's bowl.
- Check that the water is the right temperature—tepid.
- Try putting the snake in the container first, letting it settle, and then adding the water.

How to Keep a Shed

You may want to keep your snake's shed skin, especially its first one, as a milestone comparable to its first birthday. (Come on, sing it: *Happy Herpday to you. . . .*)

SNAKE BITES
Snake "boxing" is becoming popular in Thailand: people pay twenty-five cents to watch a snake handler battle a king cobra for ten minutes.

Denise Loving has experimented with many methods, and here's what she finds works best.

- Carefully unroll the shed if it is rolled up. If it has dried, dampen it with water and work with it damp.

- Wet the shed with rubbing alcohol to kill as many pathogens as possible.

- Blow into the mouth from a few inches away to inflate it.

- Use a long pin through the head to stick it to a wall or cork board, so the skin doesn't touch the wall. If it dries in contact with a smooth surface it may stick.

- Let it dry for a day or two, then hang it or lay it on a shelf for display. It can also be rolled up and stored in a plastic bag.

FOR LIZARD LOVERS
Corner shower stalls made of molded plastic are good for arboreal lizards. Just add a top and some lighting.

A word of warning: Researchers have found viable salmonella organisms on skin sheds that had been hanging in their lab for years. Dried rattlesnake meat, flesh, bones, and pills made from snake parts may also carry health risks. Therefore, employ the same health precautions when touching dry skins, or having contact with any snake parts, as when touching snakes themselves.

Snakes in the Mist

Yes, you can raise the humidity around your whole house, but if you don't like your glasses to steam up while you're reading, just raise the humidity around your snake. One way to do this is to use a plant mister to spritz the walls, floor, and ceiling of its viv several times a day.

Another purpose of misting snakes? Since shouting "Enough already" isn't going to get a snake to unwrap itself from around your arm or stick, it may be encouraged with a little mist to let go and creep away.

Some people also use a fine squirt of water when it's time to wake their pet up for dinner. But before misting a snake, remember that not every snake will tolerate a gentle squirt of water. Some will react defensively, especially if they take a direct hit. Wouldn't you?

Constipated Snakes

A plugged-up snake is an unhappy snake. So what's a pet owner to do if his or her snake has a hard feeling in the abdomen and hasn't eliminated? It's not like you can force brown rice and tofu down a poor snake's mouth.

First, you have to figure out what's causing the problems:

- Lack of exercise.

- Too much food.

- Lower cage humidity, which increases the rate of evaporative water loss, and can cause problems.

- According to Dr. John Rossi, too cool a temperature can cause the snake to "hug" its heat source, which in turn can "cook" the stool in its colon. Once the stool is dried out, it's difficult for the snake to pass it.

Things that work are:

- Giving a snake a warm bath (a standard treatment). Soak the snake in warm—not hot—water for fifteen to thirty minutes. You can do this in a plastic sweater box or Rubbermaid-type dishpan with holes in the lid.

- Daily handling.

- Skipping some feedings.

- Using an undertank heating pad for belly warmth. Be careful, because there's always a chance of these getting too hot, and a snake can die quickly from overheating. Only put the pad on one end, so the snake can escape if it warms up too much.

- Using a humidifier near the cage.

- Giving your snake an enema, but don't try this without speaking to your vet first.

Finally, speak to your vet immediately if your snake has the opposite problem: diarrhea. Although it may help to increase the environmental temperature, since the runs can be a fatal problem, you don't want to try "home remedies" for very long.

Of Rice and Men

Roger, a snake owner, tells of the time he looked into the cage of his new snake and saw a small, opaque, oblong object. He decided it was "the pupa of some hideous internal parasite," and he became upset when he noticed more and more of these as he opened his snake's cage.

The hide box was the worst. "Several more of these vile things came out with it. I had visions of the scene from *Alien*, when John Hurt has an alien being explode from his stomach." But his snake looked OK. Roger was just about to call his vet anyway, when he noticed the label on the hide box.

It said: Uncle Ben's Quick Boiled Rice.

FOR LIZARD LOVERS

Some lizards can tell the difference between closely related species of snakes. They may also imitate a snake to protect themselves. For example, when threatened by a python, a savannah monitor will put its body into a ring by grabbing its back leg with its mouth to make a circle. Since snakes usually eat their prey head first, the snake doesn't know where to begin.

Giving Snakes an Injection: Three Things to Know

- Put the injection in the front part of the snake (unless a vet tells you otherwise), or the medication could go through its kidneys, damaging them.

- When giving an injection, insert the needle at an angle, not perpendicularly. If the snake moves suddenly, it could cause the needle to penetrate too deeply and hurt it.

- Morgan Kennedy suggests you use a pillowcase and "squish" the snake down into the bottom so it can't move around. Feel for the head, and you've got the upper third of the body where you're going to give the shot. Then administer the shot right through the pillowcase.

FOR LIZARD LOVERS
People have contracted salmonella without even touching a diseased lizard. They may touch something that someone else touched, who may not have cleaned his or her hands after cleaning their lizard's cage.

The Terrarium and Vivarium

Are Hot Rocks Hot Stuff?

The consensus of pet owners of the Slither newsgroup is that snake owners should give hot rocks the cold shoulder. The concept of a snake basking on a sun-warmed rock may *seem* sound, but the use of an electrically heated surface is risky at best.

SNAKE BITES Many early settlers in America regularly ate snakes.

As much as hot rocks may add to the interior decoration of your tank, the danger they present to your snake far outweighs any cosmetic appeal. Hear are some of these dangers and problems that past users have reported:

- They get too hot and the snake can get burned. Any heating device that requires the animal to make contact for warmth is potentially risky, providing dangerously localized heat on the animal.

- They're usually too small for a snake to use to get its whole body warm, and they don't heat the whole cage.

- They sometimes short circuit, starting fires, besides burning snakes.

- Thermostats may go on the fritz and not produce any heat at all when you think they're working. This can cause potentially serious health problems for your snakes, such as respiratory difficulties.

FOR LIZARD LOVERS A chuckwalla will get inside of a crevice and expand its lungs with air, so predators can't remove it.

• They also serve as a breeding ground for bacteria that can be hazardous to both snakes and humans.

The alternative? Author Lenny Flank says:

> *Hot rocks are the work of the devil and have killed or injured many a snake. Replace it with either an incandescent heating lamp, or ceramic heat bulb (on the outside of the tank), or an undertank heater (these look like little electric blankets that stick to the bottom of the tank). The only way a hot rock is safe is if you don't plug it in.*

Since hot rocks obviously aren't so hot, what do you do if you've bought one? Cut off the cord and use it as decoration.

Snakes, Ah, Pigs in a Blanket

Most people used to think of those little hot dogs in dough when you said "pigs in a blanket." But now, with so many people collecting reptiles, the phrase conjures up something else to many. What delicacy is now hidden in the mystery of a "pig blanket"? None, unless you're a snake looking for a warm resting place.

Basically, a "pig blanket"—used by farmers to keep pigs warm, hence its name—is a sheet of insulation placed on the floor of a snake habitat. They don't actually heat an enclosure, but they do provide additional ground heat for a warm basking area. The blanket is laid out under the cage so it covers an area about one-third of the floor surface. It is then set at a temperature that produces a suitable warm surface on the bottom of the cage. An electric thermostat is used to maintain this temperature.

If the pig blanket doesn't come with a thermostat, it's recommended you buy one, which, unfortunately, can cost you as much as the blanket itself. Also, the temperature of your pig blanket must be regulated so as not to rise dangerously high. Finally, don't let the pig blanket touch the bottom of your tank, since you need to allow airflow.

Hopefully, these will make your snake as cozy and toasty as a pig in . . . well, you know.

Some Like It Cool!

Obviously, you can turn on a fan or turn off a heating apparatus to cool your snake's environment if there's a power outage. More creative ideas were suggested by Sharon Bolton, who should know because she lives in Phoenix, where the snakes aren't always "hot" but the temperature sure is:

- Use clay pots as hide boxes for your snakes, put an ice cube on top, and let it melt over it.

- Use marble. Not the round ones you roll, but marble tiles, cutting boards, coasters, etc., all of which stay cool no matter how warm the rest of the environment gets. A marble tile is a good hide box floor if your air-conditioning dies too.

- Marbles. This time it *is* the round ones you play with. Placed in a pan with a little bit of water, about halfway up, the snakes can lie on the bed of cool marbles without actually being in the water.

- Very deep potting soil, slightly damp. Good for your snake to play in if you've to get through a couple of days without power.

- Cold gel packs, kept at room temperature, can be packed around overheated snakes.

FOR LIZARD LOVERS

Geckos are the only really vocal lizard. They make squeaking, quacking, or barking sounds, depending on the species.

Heat and Light Are Not the Same

Reptiles need both heat and light for a healthy life and, as reptiles grow in popularity as pets, a proliferation of products designed to get these jobs done have hit the market. Many are more expensive than efficient.

Experienced reptile vets and herpetoculturists (aka snake experts) believe that the best source of heat for snakes in captivity is through a radiant source—not a heated rock, flexible heat tape, or heating pad.

Any incandescent bulb—be it a special reptile basking light, a silvered reflector light, or even an infrared heat lamp—can be used for daytime lighting and heating when ambient room lighting is dim, or the only other light source is fluorescent.

CHEs, or ceramic heat emitters—the best known brand is Pearlco—screw into a light fixture and provide radiant heat without light.

For nights, use dark decorative incandescent bulbs in red, blue, or green—or special reptile nightlights—that won't disrupt the sleep of your diurnal snakes or stress out your nocturnal ones.

Just make sure that the fixture you use is rated for the bulb wattage you selected, and that it is properly positioned.

Are Newspapers Good Substrates?

Snake owners have a variety of opinions on the substrate subject, and most of the information is anecdotal, often applying to just one species of snake. For example, the *Chicago Herpetological Society Bulletin* reported that a small study of Mexican lance-headed rattlesnakes, when given access to three substrates—mulch, glass, and newspapers—showed a definite preference for the mulch. (Thank you very mulch for that information.)

> **SNAKE BITES**
> Michael Jackson has an albino python.

Owners of many species prefer newspapers, which they find to be economical, clean-looking, and easy to clean. Before getting to the problems, though, here are some more pluses:

- You can see mites easily on them.

- Unlike most substrates, which snakes may ingest accidentally while going for prey, this one is not likely to get into either end of your snake.

As for safety, although one herper insists that all white paper is bleached using a process involving the use of known carcinogens, most American newspapers use soy-based ink, so at least you don't have to worry about ink toxicity.

But problems reported with newspapers as substrate include:

- They don't allow enough traction during the shedding process.

- They generally don't dry totally, and you can end up with black fingers after handling.

- If your snake goes on it, you may have to take out all the furniture, since you can't just spot clean it.

- "It's not very aesthetic if your snake likes to get wet and then crawl around," points out one owner.

By the way, paper toweling is an even more absorbent substrate than newspaper, but is much more expensive to buy and may contain more chemicals.

FOR LIZARD LOVERS
Many desert lizards have horizontal bars under their tails, creating an optical illusion that makes it difficult for predators to follow them.

Coming Clean—Does Bleach Work?

A clean and sterile cage is crucial to the health and happiness of your herp. Although a few owners claim that bleach has been implicated in different types of ailments, most use it without complaints.

The generally accepted method is to use a 5 percent solution of bleach and water, and if something needs to be disinfected, it should remain fifteen to thirty minutes. Afterward, rinse thoroughly. As one person said: "I rinse to the point of paranoia."

A Snake with a View

Your snake may not want bunk beds, a TV, or a computer, but like a child, it needs a room to call its own. This is not as easy a setup as it sounds. Nothing is more irritating than finding out that you've designed your pet's home incorrectly and have to live with that or, worse, start over.

Therefore, get it done right the first time. Caring for a snake is not as simple as people think. As Frank Gould said: "Eighty to ninety percent of people who get reptiles haven't got a clue about them and think they're as 'easy as dogs' to take care of."

They're not. Here are a few things beginning snake books sometimes forget to tell you about setting up a herp room, but *Reptile Hobbyist* wrote them up for you:

- Get a calendar to keep a record of feedings. This is especially important if you have more than one snake. Being organized in this area can ultimately be a matter of life or death.

- Have a snake stick around. Even a nonvenomous snake can deliver a good bite if surprised, awakened, hungry, irritated, or all of the above.

- Keep fresh water nearby to avoid running back and forth to the sink.

- If you use air fresheners, don't spray too close to your snake. Also, don't use stick-ups, since prolonged exposure is not good for a snake.

- Keep a magnifying glass handy to catch mites and other possible health problems before they become serious.

- A thermometer is necessary, so you'll know the exact temperature in your snake's room. In fact, some experts suggest using two: one for the cooler side, and one for the warmer one. (A thermometer should also be used for water when soaking a snake, because while 100° may feel warm to us, it's too hot for many snakes.)

- A light timer to regulate rest time from active time.

Finally, be sure that all areas of the room are completely sealed. All it takes is a small crack in a window to create a draft that will play havoc with your attempts to regulate heating.

Now if only you could get your snakes to clean up their room.

How to Clean Around a Snake

Since you can't send your herps out to play while you clean their room, you might utilize the method of one breeder of Burmese pythons. Rather than moving his big snakes to a "holding pen" for housecleaning, he coaxes his charges to one side of the cage, and slides a divider door in the middle.

After the snakeless side is cleaned, the divider is removed and the inhabitants "escorted" to their freshly spruced habitat. Then, the divider is replaced and the other side is cleaned with a minimum of handling.

It's much safer this way for you and your long, thin friend.

FOR LIZARD LOVERS
One reason lizards are often still is because they must rest their blood cells after a lot of activity.

Are Real Plants Safe in a Terrarium?

Not always. And unless you know what you're doing, you may be better off buying phony plants for your little Garden of Eden.

The problem with real plants is that there isn't much research or agreement on safe ones for snakes. Many studies have been conducted on other animals, and people, but what's nonpoisonous to a snake is not necessarily what's safe for a human or other animal, since reptiles are acutely sensitive to certain chemicals.

If you're wondering why plants can be harmful to a snake in a terrarium but not in nature, bear in mind that a snake can just crawl away from a plant in the wild. But in a terrarium, the plant stays with the snake no matter what. (Or at least until the plant dies, or the snake knocks it over often enough that the owner gets tired of picking it up and puts it elsewhere.)

SNAKE BITES
The venom of a female black widow spider is more potent than that of a rattlesnake.

By the way, some recommend bromeliads for snake cages. Although their sharp leaf edges are something to watch out for, they don't require any soil, only an occasional misting, and they're very tough, so snakes can crawl on them without killing them. But only buy those plants grown in captivity, as opposed to "wild collected," and ask the grower if they use any type of fertilizer, pest repellent, etc. Don't buy the plant if they do.

FOR LIZARD LOVERS
Most lizards are harder to keep than most snakes since they often require more room.

Should Snakes Have Roommates?

You think you have roommate problems? Your roommate drinks your Pepsi, uses your toothpaste (invariably leaving off the top), and doesn't clean his share of the dishes? Thank your lucky stars you don't have a snake as a roommate.

Some snakes in captivity when housed with other snakes will *eat* them—especially if they're smaller—because they're part of their natural menu. Even if a snake is not ordinarily cannibalistic, it may eat its roomie because it has the scent of prey on its body, and the predator mistakenly believes that its roommate is a moveable feast.

Therefore, it's generally better to provide separate habitats for nonbreeding snakes, which also prevents the problem of one snake becoming territorial and defending its space from an intruder. Keeping them apart may also reduce stress—those who have lived with a bad roommate can dig that—which in turn can lead to feeding problems. That may jeopardize its health, making it more disease prone.

FOR LIZARD LOVERS
A limb with bark on it is easier for a lizard to climb on than one that has been peeled.

Herper's Bizarre

Snakes Are Sprung!

Remember that old childhood poem: "Spring is sprung, the grass is riz" . . . yadda yadda yadda? But did you know that the second stanza was about snakes? Here it is:

> *Snakes is small,*
> *Not tall at all,*
> *They ain't even got no stature,*
> *And when they stare,*
> *They take great care*
> *To always look right ature.*

FOR LIZARD LOVERS
After eating, many lizards polish their mouths with their tongues.

My Choissss for a Pet

By Rob S. Rice
(the following is a condensed version of his poem)

> *America's number one pet, so they say,*
> *is Felis Domesticus—cat, to the lay-*
> *Man, and as I can see when I'm out on my jobs*
> *There are bunches of folks still who put up with dogs.*
> . . . .
> *Which brings up the case that I'd now like to make—*
> *There's not a pet here I'd prefer to a snake!*
> *A python, or boa, or corn snake, no matter,*
> *Perhaps a black rat snake, or a friendly puff adder . . .*
>
> *Stop sweating and shaking! You'll scroll off the page!*
> *Do not yield to loathing, revulsion or rage!*
> *Your ophidophobia can wait for a while,*
> *So please pay attention to this herpophile.*

Consider snake—housing-a sock will suffice
(But not in the sock drawer, now that's good advice).
No barking, or yowling, or petulant squawks!
No need for a leash when you take snake for walks!

Now, mice are a problem, and face it, the cat
If it deigns to stalk them, or notice that
They've torn things to ribbons, and chases at all
Is balked and then laughed at by mice in the wall!

But now take your reptile—the rodent's enholed,
And thinking it's safe well entrenched in the mould-
ing, but then it finds out what we snake lovers know:
There's no place for mice where a snake cannot go!
. . . .
If you like it when dogs fawn, the cat rubs your leg,
The parrot says "Feed me," but notice, I beg
That though others slobber you, greet and then chase you,
It's only the snake who's equipped to embrace you.

You're pestered by salesmen or fear a housebreaker?
Your serpent will fright such more than his maker!
It gropes for the silver and loses his mind
When "Fido," your python, has got it entwined!

A snake never acts like it's scared or excited.
It won't plague your table when it's not invited.
There's plenty of room if it's sharing your bed.
And triple-damned shedding won't stop up your head!

I could go on for ages (and went, it might seem)
And I do admit serpents might not suit the squeam-
ish, but think on a reptile, and remember that
Your snake thinks far better of you than your cat!

FOR LIZARD LOVERS
A horned lizard can squirt blood from his eyes up to seven feet away.

You Might Be a Herper If . . .

(Jim Sullivan started this humorous list on the Internet, and then many contributed to it.)

You might be a herper if . . .

> Upon seeing the famous photo of a model naked with a boa constrictor around her, your first reaction is, "Nice-looking snake."
>
> You watch *Crocodile Dundee, Raiders of the Lost Ark*, etc., and root for the reptiles instead of the hero.
>
> You get a sunburn and worry that your shed isn't coming off in one piece.
>
> You have twenty-seven dog and cat bowls around and no dogs or cats.
>
> You go to the zoo or pet store to try to find a date.
>
> People nervously look at your wrists and begin to hide sharp implements.
>
> When a person is described as "a real snake in the grass," you think you'd really enjoy meeting them.
>
> You find out who your real friends are because they're the only ones who are willing to ask you how your day was over lunch.
>
> Redecorating the house means finding a way to squeeze in another vivarium.
>
> You use the word *shed* a lot and aren't referring to an outbuilding on your property.
>
> Your wife remarks: "I'm not doing the laundry again until you find it!"
>
> Your house is on the robbery list—to be avoided at all costs!
>
> Your relatives make elaborate excuses to avoid visiting your place.
>
> The photos of loved ones in your wallet look like lobby stills from *Jurassic Park*.
>
> You have friends over for dinner, and someone notices the vermicelli is moving.

Snake Sources

Bibliography

Flank, Lenny Jr. *Herp Help.* New York: Howell Book House, 1992.

———. *Snakes: Their Care and Keeping.* New York: Howell Book House, 1998.

———. *The Snake: An Owner's Guide to a Happy Healthy Pet.* New York: Howell Book House, 1996.

Greene, Harry W. *Snakes. The Evolution of Mystery in Nature.* Berkeley, California: University of California Press, 1997.

Grenard, Steve. *Medical Herpetology.* Pottsville, Pennsylvania: Reptile & Amphibian, 1994.

Griehl, Klaus. *Snakes: Giant Snakes and Non-Venomous Snakes in the Terrarium.* Hauppauge, New York: Barron's, 1982.

Hanson, Jeanne K. *The Beastly Book: 100 of the World's Most Dangerous Creatures.* New York: Prentice Hall General Reference, 1993.

Linley, Mike. *Weird & Wonderful Snakes.* New York: Thomson Learning, 1993.

Llewellyn, Claire. *I Didn't Know That Some Snakes Spit Poison.* Brookfield, Connecticut: Copper Beech Books, 1997.

Lovett, Sarah. *Extremely Weird Snakes.* Santa Fe, New Mexico: John Muir Publications, 1993.

Matthews, Peter, ed. *The Guinness Book of Records.* New York: Bantam, 1994.

Mattison, Chris. *Snakes of the World.* New York: Facts on File, 1986.

———. *The Encyclopedia of Snakes.* New York: Facts on File, 1995.

Obstfeld, Raymond. *Kinky Cats, Immortal Amoebas, and Nine-armed Octopuses.* New York: HarperCollins, 1997.

Roever, J. M. *Snake Secrets.* New York: Walker & Co., 1979.

Rossi, John, D.V.M., M.A. and Roxanne Rossi. *What's Wrong with My Snake?* Sanatee, California: Advanced Vivarium Systems, Inc., 1996.

Tulin, Melissa S. *Aardvarks to Zebras.* New York: A Citadel Press Book, 1995.

Magazines

Reptiles
P.O. Box 58700
Boulder, Colorado 80322
(800) 321-1000
$27.97 a year
http://animalnetwork.com/reptiles/default.asp

Reptile Hobbyist
TFH Publications Inc.
1 TFH Plaza
Neptune City, New Jersey 07753
(732) 988-8400
$40 a year
http://www.tfh.com

The Vivarium
1924 Mission Road
Suite N/P
Escondido, California 92029
(800) 982-9410
$28 a year
http://www.thevivarium.com/index.htm

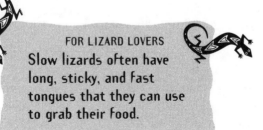

FOR LIZARD LOVERS
Slow lizards often have long, sticky, and fast tongues that they can use to grab their food.

Websites

rec.pets.herp FAQ
http://www.landfield.com/faqs/pets/herp-faq/part1
http://www.landfield.com/faqs/pets/herp-faq/part2
http://www.landfield.com/faqs/pets/herp-faq/part3

website of the Discovery Channel
http://www.discovery.com

King Cobra page on the National Geographic magazine website
http://www.nationalgeographic.com/kingcobra/index-n.html

National Animal of Poison Control Center
http://www.napcc.aspca.org/

Herp Care Collection (Melissa Kaplan)
http://www.sonic.net/melissk/

Quake! Living on the Fault Line (Melissa Kaplan)
http://www.sonic.net/daltons/melissa/quake.html

You might be a herper if . . .
http://www.sonic.net/melissk/youmight.html

Lenny Flank's Herp Page
http://www.geocities.com/RainForest/2421

Medical Herpetology (Steve Grenard)
http://www.xmission.com/~gastown/herpmed/medherp.htm

Reptile-Associated Salmonellosis Information Page (Steve Grenard)
http://www.xmission.com/~gastown/herpmed/salm.htm

Welcome to the Wild Kingdom (Morgan Kennedy)
http://home.earthlink.net/~snakegirl/

Erik's Snakepage! (Erik Stenström)
http://stud.sb.luth.se/~eriste-6/index.html

Transporting Venomous Snakes (Allen Hunter)
http://stud.sb.luth.se/~eriste-6/hots3.html

Dave Fulton's website
http://www.thenet.co.uk/~davefulton/

The Pink Python (Ray Miller)
http://home.clara.net/rmns/rept1.htm

Bayou Bob's Brazos River Rattlesnake Ranch
http://www.wf.net/~snake

For websites of major magazines, see p. 171

Slither mailing list
If you wish to subscribe to this list, e-mail owner Terry Kirk at
python@slither.com.

FOR LIZARD LOVERS
Some lizards defecate in
their water pools, so you must
change their water frequently.

Lizard Sources

Bibliography

Coborn, John. *Lizards as a New Pet*. Neptune City, New Jersey: TFH, 1992.

De Vosjoli, Phillippe. *The General Care and Maintenance of Green Water Dragons, Sailfin Lizards, and Basilisks*. Lakeside, California: Advanced Vivarium Systems, 1992.

Flank, Lenny, Jr. *Herp Help*. New York: Howell Book House, 1998.

Jes, Harald. *Lizards in the Terrarium*. Hauppauge, NY: Barron's Educational Series, 1987.

McKeown, Sean. *The General Care and Maintenance of Day Geckos*. Lakeside, California: Advanced Vivarium Systems, 1996.

Richardson, Maurice Lane. *The Fascination of Reptiles*. New York: Hill and Wang, 1972.

Sprackland, Robert G. Jr. *All About Lizards*. Neptune City, New Jersey: TFH, 1977.

Magazines

Reptiles (see page 171)

Websites

rec.pets.herp
http://www.sonic.net/melissk (Melissa Kaplan's page)

FOR LIZARD LOVERS
A lizard lover in Los Angeles has changed his name to Henry Lizardlover.

About the Author

Paulette Cooper is the author of twelve books and over 1,000 articles. Her pet books include *277 Secrets Your Dog Wants You to Know* and *277 Secrets Your Cat Wants You to Know*. The latter won the Muse Award for the Best Cat Book (category, other) in 1998. Besides that award, she has won four other writing awards. Paulette's other books include *The Medical Detectives* and *The Scandal of Scientology*. All together, her books have sold close to a half a million copies.

Paulette is a member of the prestigious American Society of Journalists & Authors and is listed in Who's Who in America. She holds a B.A. with Honors from Brandeis University and an M.A. from City University in Psychology.

Her husband, Paul Noble, who co-authors some of her books, is Director of Feature Films at Lifetime Television. They live in New York with two dogs and have owned three cats and three birds.

Snake Index

Lizard Index

More from Paulette Cooper!

277 Secrets Your Dog Wants You to Know
(with Paul Noble)
$8.95, ISBN 1-58008-014-6
5.5 x 8.5 inches, 208 pages

• Is it safe to let your dog kiss you? • Stopping dogs' thunder fears • What do dogs think about? • Do dogs get VD? • Embarrassing behavior of your dog • Six diseases you can give your dog (and sixty he can give you) • Are dogs psychic? • Nine people foods you should never feed your dog • Does your dog need Prozac? • Is alcohol or marijuana safe for your dog? • The O.J. Simpson case: What the Akita knows • The five most difficult dogs to own • Should you vacuum your dog? • Do rawhide chews work? • Does your smoking hurt your dog? • Save your dog with the Heimlich maneuver • New pills that stop your older dog from acting it • Nineteen products that could save your dog's life • Nonshock gadget stops dogs from barking • Ninety little-known dangers that could kill your dog • Publications that may print photos of your dog • How to stop a dog from biting you or your child • The most expensive gifts for dogs • And much, much more!

277 Secrets Your Cat Wants You to Know
(with Paul Noble)
$8.95, ISBN 0-89815-952-0
5.5 x 8.5 inches, 256 pages

Ten ways to get your cat to love you more • Seven secret signs your cat will attack—and four ways to stop it • Cats who stop using the litter box—and what to do • Fifteen things that stop your cat from misbehaving • Getting cats to stop scratching the furniture and waking you up • Saving money on cat food, litter, vet bills, flea medicine & grooming • Stopping your cat from spraying • Fifteen ways your cat shows she likes you • Eight weird things cats eat or lick • Cats who bite themselves • Handling finicky eaters and hunger strikes • Five things to look for on any pet food label • What every cat allergy sufferer should know • Offbeat ways to stop your two cats from fighting • Seventy-one ways to save your cat's life • Spotting cat cancer signs • Best flea products (and common ones that can kill cats) • Keeping cats from plants and soils • Introducing a second cat to yours • How to talk to your cat • What your cat is trying to say to you • Do cats go to heaven? • And much, much more!

Available from your local bookstore, or by ordering direct from the publisher.
Write for our catalogs of over 1,000 books, posters, and tapes.

TEN SPEED PRESS • CELESTIAL ARTS • TRICYCLE PRESS
Box 7123, Berkeley, California 94707
Order phone (800) 841-2665 • Fax (510) 559-1629
order@tenspeed.com • www.tenspeed.com